Surviving to Thriving

The MindfulEatery Dream

The MindfulEatery is my life's work in action. Grounded in my experiential philosophy, *The Energy Within ME,* it's the awareness of how consumption shapes our vitality. Energy drives motion through two forces: Love (+) and Fear (-). We gain or lose it via three pillars — *Food, Thought, and Environment* — which either support health and harmony or drain them.

Live foods nourish; dead foods deplete. Empowering thoughts uplift; draining ones confine. Harmonious environments connect; disharmonious ones isolate. *This Law of Consumption* precedes attraction: what we take in shapes what we draw. Life is choice — always changing — and our choices feed Authentic Intelligence rooted in love or artificial patterns that keep us asleep.

For over 15 years, I've envisioned transforming the upper floors of Shawbucks — my Jamestown, NY, restaurant and hub since 1995 — into a dedicated MindfulEatery. The second floor will become a healthy-eating restaurant and gathering space: nourishing meals aligned with the pillars, workshops and events, and a sanctuary for those "written off" or told they couldn't thrive.

My journey — surviving cancer right after leasing the building, turning bipolar challenges into triumphs, defying lifelong limitation predictions — shows we're not defined by others' fears or our own. We can break free and live fully.

Book proceeds will fund this dream: a real-world space for mindful nourishment, energy rediscovery, and life-affirming choices. Your purchase supports a movement for people, planet, and purposeful profit.

Thank you for joining The Energy Within ME.

Lone Star Rising

Lone Star Rising

The Energy Within ME
Choosing Love Over Fear

Kurt B Johnson

KBJ

For permission requests, contact the publisher at:

Kurt B. Johnson
Jamestown, NY
hello@kurtbjohnson.com
www.kurtbjohnson.com

First Edition

ISBN: 979-8-9951217-0-1

Printed in the United States of America

Cover and interior design by Adam Bies / Hard Rock Brand

Voices of Support

"Lone Star Rising *isn't just a book — it's a journey. I had the privilege of riding alongside Kurt on the road to Texas, and I can tell you first-hand that his story is as real as it gets. Whenever I think of Jamestown, I think of Kurt and Jimmy — two souls who lived with passion, purpose, and a love for life that's contagious.*

Kurt's words capture the spirit of adventure, brotherhood, and the kind of friendship that picks right up where it left off, no matter how much time has passed. This book is a testament to that bond — a true and authentic friendship that will last forever.

If you're looking for a story that inspires you to live fully and love deeply, Lone Star Rising *is it.*"

- Joe Cala
Longtime friend and road-trip instigator, and now
family man who shared the journey to Texas with me

"*I've known Kurt B. Johnson since we were wild kids with big dreams and no brakes. Kurt, Dave, Jimmy, and I — we were a crew, bonded by brotherhood and a shared love for life's adventures. Dave and Jimmy kept us in check, but Kurt and I? We were the ones pushing the limits, always chasing the next thrill.*

I'll never forget the day I traded my 1969 Cougar for Kurt's motorcycle. That bike had stories even after I got it from Kurt, like the time my wife, Sara, burned her leg on the exhaust. But that's how life was with Kurt —full of stories, full of heart.

Reading Lone Star Rising *brought back all those memories, but it also showed me a side of Kurt I never fully understood. Behind the laughter and the wild rides was a man carrying more than any of us knew. This book isn't just his story — it's our story. It's about friendship, resilience, and the power of choosing love over fear.*

If you've ever had a friend who changed your life, you'll find yourself in these pages. Kurt's journey is a testament to the bonds that never break, no matter how many miles or years pass. I'm proud to call him my brother, and even prouder to see him share his truth with the world.

Read this book. It'll remind you of the power of friendship, the beauty of second chances, and the courage it takes to rise."

- Bart Schuver
Brother in spirit and co-pilot in adventure

"I finished the book — you aced it! It kept my interest throughout. I started crying toward the end; it touched me, and I suddenly felt a sense of relief from the resistance I was holding on to. You were clearly intuitive from a young age, and your journey took you where you were meant to go. There are so many wonderful lessons here for your readers. It's a bestseller!"

- Sara Schuver
Wife of my oldest friend, Bart, survivor of our
youthful troubles (and that motorcycle burn)

"It was Buddhist meditation that brought Kurt and me together. I am the Dharma Leader of a local sangha, and Kurt began joining our weekly meditation sessions. As I got to know him, I saw him as one of

the most driven spiritual seekers I have ever met. Every conversation I have ever had with him is steeped in vigilance for, and devotion to, the ineffable spaciousness of our collective consciousness.

In time, our relationship resulted in a shared enterprise, Rolling Hills Radio. *The partnership between the show and Kurt's legendary business establishment, Shawbucks, clicked and took off to heights we had not imagined, in no small measure because of Kurt's business savvy, persistence, and most of all, his irresistibly contagious positive nature. In its 10-year run, 17 Grammy winners and nominees graced the Rolling Hills stage, including Lifetime Grammy winner Tom Paxton. Kurt's energy was crucial in making this happen, and his story here lingered long after the last note faded. Kurt adds this to his already impressive legacy.*

Lone Star Rising *is a fascinating read on several levels. As an autobiography, it is an inspiration — the tale of the unique man who lived this exhilarating story. He went through trying times. Very trying times. He pulls no punches recounting the entire saga with courage and honesty: the good, the bad, and the (sorry, no spoilers here).*

A noteworthy portion of the book is devoted to his personal belief system, one of compassion, choice, love, and positive living. It's a message worth hearing and taking to heart. Kurt lives it every day, every moment.

As I read this book, I wondered if people might be inspired to see their lives as a story, too. Because they are. Maybe Kurt provided the spark to help people see and appreciate that. So, I suggest everyone who reads Kurt's book write their own. Don't try to go on Kurt's journey, though.

There's nothing quite like his."

- Ken Hardley
Dharma leader, psychologist, creator and host of *Rolling Hills Radio,* musician.

"Lone Star Rising *is a courageous and deeply human story about choice — how fear shapes us, and how love ultimately frees us. Kurt B. Johnson offers a raw, reflective journey that reminds us transformation is not found in theory, but in lived experience. This book invites readers to meet themselves honestly and choose differently."*

- Micheline Nader
Bestselling author of *LEAP Beyond AI*,
LEAP Beyond Success, and *The Dolphin's Dance*

"In his new book Lone Star Rising, *Kurt B. Johnson shows us that it's never too late to transform our lives when we choose love over fear. Kurt reminds us that the same energy that lights up the sky and moves the oceans is inside all of us. It's what he calls* The Energy Within ME. *Not only will Kurt's story inspire you, but it may even cause you to see the greatest power and potential within yourself and everyone else you meet on your life's journey."*

- Drew Scott Pearlman
Filmmaker and author — director of wellness documentaries
Fuel Your Health, The Great Lesson, and *The Healing Effect,* and
author of *The Four Faces of Transformation*

"Kurt Johnson's book Lone Star Rising *is a path to wellness, one that he has personally come to understand, that he lives himself, and that he shares with his readers. He points out the importance of family, friends, and community, including teachers, in one's overall development into a fulfilled person. Commitment, courage, compassion, connections, empathy, and the belief in a spiritual life are also critical to strive for an attainable goal. He reinforces the important connection between mind, body, and spirit, and the need to nourish all three to achieve balance.*

Readers will also learn that various issues stand in the way of true wellness. Fear, the use of drugs and alcohol, and most certainly the misuse of drugs and alcohol are important obstacles to well-being, balance, and peace.

The book highlights the importance of meditation. The author gives readers the example of focusing on the Texan star. Concentrating on the star or a substitute (for example, a sunset or an image of a loved one) to the exclusion of all other thoughts is very important for calming the mind. It is also very beneficial to meditate deeply and tap into the universal energy that connects all in our universe. Negative thoughts disappear, and with practice, a feeling of peace, calmness, and safety emerges from the quiet mind. This immersion into a universal energy is a form of deep meditation and can induce feelings of peace, love, and belonging.

Most importantly, this book is a personal tribute to growth, resiliency, and transformation. It explains the emergence of a holism which rises from confusion, trauma, and adverse experiences. It points a path that begins when one is adrift and lost, leading to the evolution of a stronger, resilient, and wholesome person. From a place of darkness, Kurt teaches others the path to health, wellness, and happiness. This book will be helpful to those finding their own way to a balanced and productive life. They will come to know themselves and then help others."

- **Lillian Vitanza Ney, MD**

Retired cardiologist, medical director, and vice president of WCA Hospital, Jamestown, New York. Former coordinator of Jamestown Area Medical Association, interim acting medical director of Heritage Park Health Care Center, and former acting county health commissioner for the Chautauqua County Health Department.

"Lone Star Rising *is a story of the recovery, redemption, and renewal made possible through love. Kurt Johnson's story provides hope for those who have struggled and inspiration for those who have a vision to make a difference. I can't wait to experience his dream of the* MindfulEatery*."*

- **David Egner**

President & CEO, The Ralph C. Wilson, Jr. Foundation

"I have known Kurt Johnson since high school and have followed his journey with genuine respect. Lone Star Rising *represents more than a personal story. It stands as a meaningful contribution to our community's continued growth.*

Kurt understands the power of storytelling to bring people together, foster understanding, and inspire progress. His vision for the MindfulEatery *at Shawbucks, along with the experiential learning spaces planned for the upper floors, reflects a thoughtful commitment to community development. This initiative goes beyond food service. It is designed to create environments where individuals can learn, collaborate, and build lasting connections.*

As Mayor, I've always believed in choosing people over politics. Kurt's vision aligns perfectly with that principle — he chooses love over fear, and that choice is the most important one we can make as a community. Experiential learning will play an important role in preparing us for the future, and Kurt's leadership is helping move that vision forward. I am proud to support Kurt Johnson and Lone Star Rising *and the positive impact it will have on Jamestown and beyond."*

- Kim Ecklund
Mayor of Jamestown, NY

"As an educator and former Academic Dean, I have helped both students and colleagues find their voice. But rarely do I encounter a voice as clear and necessary as Kurt B. Johnson's.

Lone Star Rising *is not just a book—it is a testament to the power of inner discovery and the courage to follow one's true path. It is honest, authentic, and reflective.*

When Kurt first shared his writings with me, I knew there was one story that needed to be told above all others. That story became

Lone Star Rising. *It is a journey of the heart and a thoughtful framework for living with intention.*

Kurt's work is a gift to readers and a guide to those seeking their own inner compass. I am proud to have played a small part in bringing this book to life."

- **Maria Kindberg**
Retired Jamestown Community College Foundation
executive director, academic dean, and writing instructor.

"Kurt's compelling account is a reminder to each of us of the importance of living every day to the fullest, and realizing that every choice we make matters. We truly are the heroes in our own respective stories and are responsible for finding that balance of body, mind, and spirit in our own lives. A must-read for anyone searching for a bit of direction or motivation, told by a person brave enough to share his story with us."

- **Chris Olsen**
Producer and attorney, author of *Lucy Comes Home,*
board member, Robert H. Jackson Center, Jamestown, NY

"I've read Lone Star Rising *more than once, and each time, it speaks to me in a deeper way. This isn't just a book — it's a map to the promised land within us. My buddy Kurt has captured the essence of* Binary Harmetics *— the language of the heart, the cycles of expansion and contraction, and the journey of returning to oneself.*

As someone raised in Christian Science, I recognize the truth in these pages. Kurt's story is raw, real, and transformative. He doesn't just tell you about the path — he walks it, stumbles, rises, and invites you to do the same.

I've witnessed Kurt's ups and downs, and I've seen firsthand the power of his teachings. This book is a testament to resilience, authenticity, and the unwavering belief that we all carry the light within us.

If you're ready to embark on a journey of self-discovery and emotional mastery, Lone Star Rising *is your guide. It's not just a story — it's a call to remember who you are."*

- Matt Hartweg
Retired businessman, longtime golf buddy

"I've spent over a decade at the door of Shawbucks, watching the world walk in and out. I've seen the best and the worst of people, and I've learned one thing: you've got to be tough if you're going to be stupid — or make smarter choices.

And then there's Kurt B. Johnson.

I've watched Kurt handle more difficult situations than most people could imagine. He didn't just run a bar — he ran a sanctuary, a place where people could come to find themselves, even when they didn't know they were lost.

Lone Star Rising *isn't just a book. It's a testament to resilience, to making the hard choices, and to rising above the chaos. Kurt didn't just rebuild a burned-out building — he rebuilt a community. And he did it while fighting battles most people never knew about.*

I've been proud to stand by his side, to watch him turn Shawbucks into a beacon of hope. And now, with the MindfulEatery *project, he's taking it to the next level — bringing food, thought, and environment together in a way that will change lives.*

If you want to know what it means to be tough, to be smart, and to never give up, read this book. Kurt's story will inspire you to make better choices — and to stand strong, no matter what life throws your way.

It's an honor to call him my friend."

- George Wright
Retired Pepsi salesman, longtime doorman at Shawbucks

"I've known Kurt B. Johnson since we were kids — me, Kurt, Bart Schuver, and Jimmy Ross. We were inseparable, especially in high school. While I was the grounded one, Kurt was always the free spirit, chasing dreams and living life on his own terms. But after reading Lone Star Rising, *I realized there was so much more beneath the surface — things I never knew he endured, especially from his Texas experience. It's crazy how fast things can snowball out of control into the unthinkable!*

This book opened my eyes to the silent battles Kurt fought while still showing up for everyone else. It's raw, it's real, and it's a testament to the power of choosing love over fear. Kurt's story isn't just inspiring — it's a reminder that even the strongest among us carry scars we never see.

As someone who's been by his side through thick and thin, I can say this: Lone Star Rising *isn't just a memoir — it's a mirror. It reflects the resilience, courage, and grace that Kurt has always embodied, even when the world wasn't watching.*

If you want to read a story that will move you, challenge you, and remind you of what truly matters, this is it. I'm proud to call Kurt my friend, and even prouder to see him share his truth with the world."

- David Jones
Lifelong friend and conscience keeper

"I've known Kurt for decades — his wife Tammy was my college roommate and close friend. I remember Kurt teaching me to dive when I was just in ninth grade. Even then, he had a way of seeing the world differently.

A year ago, I helped Kurt organize thousands of pages of his handwritten notes — yellow legal pads filled with thoughts I couldn't fully grasp at the time. But now, seeing those pages transformed into

Lone Star Rising, *I finally understand. This book isn't just a story; it's a revelation.*

As a retired school teacher, I've read many things, but nothing quite like this. Kurt's journey from chaos to clarity is a testament to resilience and the power of storytelling. It's a gift to anyone seeking to make sense of their own life.

I'm proud to have played a small part in bringing this book to life, and I'm even prouder to call Kurt and Tammy my friends."

- Christine Yocum
Retired teacher, Friday happy-hour bartender at Shawbucks

"I've known Kurt for years — as a friend, a golfing buddy, and a visionary. But reading Lone Star Rising *opened my eyes to a part of his story I never knew. It's not just a book; it's a revelation.*

Kurt's journey through Texas taught him something profound: emotions aren't disorders — they're data. They guide us back to love. This insight alone is worth the read, especially in a world that often pathologizes feeling instead of honoring it.

As a community leader, I've always believed in unity within the community. This book embodies that spirit. It's about healing, connection, and the courage to transform personal pain into collective wisdom.

If you're looking for a story that inspires, challenges, and ultimately uplifts, Lone Star Rising *is it. Kurt doesn't just tell his story — he invites you to find your own."*

- John Felton
CEO, Southern Chautauqua Federal Credit Union

"I've known Kurt B. Johnson since before the world knew his name. We grew up in the same neighborhood, shared dreams in Dallas, and

walked through life's storms together. I've seen him at his highest highs and his deepest valleys. I've watched him rise — not just to survive, but to transform.

Lone Star Rising *isn't just a book to me. It's a testament to a life lived with courage, grace, and relentless love. Kurt doesn't just write about choosing love over fear — he lives it. I've seen him make that choice again and again, even when it cost him everything.*

This book is raw, real, and deeply inspiring. It's not just for those who know him — it's for anyone who's ever faced a crossroads and wondered which path to take. Kurt shows us that the path of love is always worth it, even when it's the hardest one.

If you want to read a story that will move you, challenge you, and remind you of what truly matters, Lone Star Rising *is that story. I'm proud to call Kurt my friend, and even prouder to see him share his light with the world."*

- **Tom Brigiotta**
Lifelong friend and witness to the journey

"Our community knows me as the head of Artone Manufacturing, one of the largest hospitality manufacturers in the USA. But to me, the real honor is being Kurt B. Johnson's friend.

We've shared more than business — we've shared wisdom, dreams, and the kind of conversations you can only have with someone who truly gets it. Kurt designed his own desk, and we built it. We crafted cabinets for Shawbucks.

But what I didn't know — what Lone Star Rising *revealed to me — was the depth of his journey.*

I knew Kurt was best friends with Jimmy, Ross, and Joe Cala. I knew he built Shawbucks while battling chemotherapy. But I never knew the horrors he endured in Texas — the crucible that forged his resilience. Now I understand how he could take a building destroyed by fire and turn it into Shawbucks — a Phoenix rising from the ashes.

Kurt's insight and creative genius as an architect are unmatched. But it's his heart, his ability to move forward when everything seems impossible, that truly inspires me.

This book is not just his story — it's a testament to the power of friendship, resilience, and the human spirit. It's an honor to call Kurt my friend, to share this life, and to raise a glass with him on my way home from work.

If you want to understand what it means to rebuild from nothing, to rise from the ashes, read Lone Star Rising. *Kurt's story will change you."*

- **Mike Calimeri**
Owner & President, Artone Manufacturing

"Dude, you laid it all out. Nice background history. You bring us back to our youth. A time of invincibility, promise, and hope. Then slap us to the ground where youth and truth collide. Hello darkness, my old friend. In the pit, looking up toward the light, but no ladder in sight. Surrender. Rise like the phoenix from the fire. Some not so successful. Roads paved and roads that ended too soon. Picked the road less traveled, knowing you would never pass that fork again. A personal journey any Jamestown boy can relate to. Been there, bro. The other side of sanity and back, but somehow settling in the middle. I remember getting out of the army in 86' and seeing you at the end of the bar at the Grog, in your usual spot, silent, stoic, a man of few words. Now I know the story, not long from the fall. Left me wanting to know more, another 50 pages, wife, kids, cancer, death, success. But then again, I have the gift of knowing you and can call you a friend. Love ya' bro."

- **Chris Merchant**
Old friend, retired owner of Mariner's Pier Restaurant on Chautauqua Lake.

"Wow! I just finished your book, and I'm not a reader. I wanted to keep reading. I recognize this book as the natural expression of your journey. It offers a clear, compassionate framework for choosing love over fear — one that feels lived, not learned, through all your life experiences. It carries the weight of lived experience and invites the reader to practice, not just believe. What an incredible and interesting journey. I think you need to continue with more chapters about your life today and your many successes. Your positive energy and your choice to love over fear have made you who you are today. Thank you for letting me read this. I will certainly promote this read."

- Teresa Isabella

A cherished close family friend, my very first *Vital Mind Reset* student, a courageous cancer survivor, a dedicated elementary school teacher, and mother to our sons' best friend.

"I've skated on ice in the Olympics, played pro hockey across Europe, and met people from all walks of life. But nothing prepared me for the kind of friendship I found with Kurt B. Johnson.

We met in 2018 when the Rebels Hockey team moved to Jamestown Northwest Arena. Joe Coombs, the head coach, asked Kurt to take me golfing at Moonbrook Country Club. By the time we teed off, we were already best friends. It was like meeting a brother I didn't know I had.

Kurt's story is one of resilience, vision, and heart. He's faced more than most people could handle, yet he's come out stronger, not just for himself, but for everyone around him. He doesn't just rebuild buildings — he rebuilds communities, and he does it with a contagious spirit.

Lone Star Rising *isn't just a book — it's a testament to what happens when you refuse to give up, even when everything around you is burning. It's about finding your breath, your purpose, and your people, even in the darkest times.*

I've heard Kurt's story before, but never in this detail. And let me tell you, it hits home. It's raw, it's real, and it's inspiring. If you're looking for a story that will lift you up and remind you of what's possible, this is it.

Kurt, you're not just a friend —you're family. And this book is a gift to everyone who reads it."

- Pat Dunn
Former 1993 Olympic hockey player for France,
professional hockey veteran, and friend.

"I'm Boom Briggs, owner of 99B Race Team in the World of Outlaws Series. I've spent my life in the racing and trucking business, riding the highs and lows, the wins and losses. And if there's one thing I've learned, it's that life isn't just about winning — it's about learning. The real lessons come when you don't take the checkered flag, but those lessons prepare you for the next race.

I watched many of Kurt's Mindful Mondays. *They've been a guiding insight for me, even when I didn't know I needed one. And now, with* Lone Star Rising, *I finally understand where his philosophy began. This book is filled with resilience, love, and the power of choice.*

Kurt's journey mirrors the track: unpredictable, challenging, but always moving forward. I'm proud to call him a friend and honored to endorse Lone Star Rising. *It's a book for anyone who's ever faced a tough lap and kept going."*

- Boom Briggs
Driver and team owner, 99B Race Team – World of Outlaws Series

"I'm John Lobb — 28L on the track, and a lifetime racer at heart. I've spent my youth tearing up dirt tracks and making memories at Shawbucks. Those were the days — fast cars, late nights, and friendships that felt like family.

When I read Lone Star Rising, *it hit me hard. Kurt's story wasn't just his — it was mine too. I remember going four days without sleep, chasing something I couldn't name. Racing taught me that life is a mirror. Every lap reflects your choices, your fears, your courage.*

Kurt's book reminded me that even when you're spinning out, there's a lesson in the skid. It's not about how fast you go — it's about how you handle the turns. Lone Star Rising *is a testament to resilience, to finding your way back even when the lights go out.*

I'm proud to stand with Kurt and endorse this book. It's for anyone who's ever raced, loved, lost, and found themselves again."

- John Lobb
Retired World of Outlaws racer

"We are the Dick Barton 28B Race Team — a brotherhood forged in the heat of competition and the camaraderie of Tuesday nights at Shawbucks. Over the years, we've learned that racing isn't just about speed — it's about heart, resilience, and the will to rise again after every setback.

Lone Star Rising *is more than a book to us. It's a reflection of the journey we've all taken together. Kurt's story mirrors the highs and lows of racing: the thrill of victory, the sting of defeat, and the unwavering drive to keep moving forward.*

This book captures the essence of what it means to be part of a team, to push through the adversity, and never to give up — no matter how many laps it takes.

Kurt's story is our story. It's about finding strength in friendships, community, and connections. It's about realizing that we are all part of something bigger.

We dedicate this endorsement to the memory of Ron Nielson, the late owner of the 28B tram and Raceway 7. Ron was more than our car owner. He was a builder of dreams and a respected pillar in the racing community. His legacy lives on in every racing story we tell.

We proudly endorse Lone Star Rising *as a testament to the power of friendship, perseverance, and the unbreakable spirit of those who dare to dream."*

- The Dick Barton 28B Race Team
Racing team of National Dirt Late Model Hall of Fame driver Dick Barton

"I'm Chub Frank — known on the track as 1. I've spent my life racing Dirt Late Models against the best in the world. I met Kurt back in the late '90s when he owned the 01 car for my good friend John Venable II. We lost John too soon, and we lost my wife Mary too soon. Racing teaches you about loss, grit, and the power of community.*

Kurt's book, Lone Star Rising, *isn't just another story — it's a testament to resilience. It's about choosing love over fear, and finding the star within you, even when the track goes dark. Kurt suffered pains and struggles most of us never saw. But he learned that 'The only bad experience is the one you didn't learn from.'*

This book is for every racer, every fan, and every person who's ever faced a tough lap. It's about rising, no matter how many times you spin out.

I'm proud to call him a friend, and I'm honored to endorse Lone Star Rising."

- Chub Frank
World-renowned dirt late model driver

To Jimmy Ross

Born January 10, 1964 – Passed June 12, 1986

This book is dedicated to my dear friend Jimmy Ross, whose light burned brightly but far too briefly. Though your time here was short, your impact was profound. You taught me the value of laughter, loyalty, and living fully in the moment. Your spirit continues to inspire me every day.

In these pages, I carry forward the lessons we shared and the dreams we spoke of. This work is a tribute to your memory and a promise that your legacy lives on through every word.

You are missed, but never forgotten.

Appreciation

A heartfelt thanks to all who supported this journey

To my friend Adam Bies, whom I met in August 2024 during his tough times. You stepped up to build out my websites, help edit this book, design the cover, and handle all the text formatting and interior layout. Your talent and dedication made this book beautiful. I can't thank you enough.

To KN Literary for connecting me with the editor of this book, Zach Hively. Zach, your sharp edits, thoughtful guidance, and expertise shaped this manuscript perfectly. I truly appreciate everything you did. Thank you!

To Gavin Paterniti, who helped me edit the original version of this *Texas Story* back in 2018, and brought early insight to my writing. As a talented musician who performs at Shawbucks, you've been part of the community that continues to inspire me. Thank you for your help back then — and for everything since.

To Walt Pickett, my first editor for the 2014 book proposal we sent to the Hay House Writers Workshop, titled *Forgiveness of Fear: Live to Love, Die from Fear.* Your guidance as a writer and editor set the foundation for me to finally write this book. Thank you!

To my friend Dr. Ken Erickson, who sparked my writing journey over lunch with his question, "Why write a book? Everything's been said before." After a good laugh, you continued,

"Everything's been said before, just not by you, in your voice." Your simple formula of *Tell them what you're going to say, say it, and then tell them what you said,* gave me freedom and structure. Thank you, my friend.

To my friend Gary Padak, PhD, whom I met at Jamestown Rotary in 2015. As a retired literature professor and dean, you read my early work about my *MindfulEatery* project, and gave me the word "consume" for the *Law of Consumption — Food, Thoughts, Environment.* Your wisdom meant a lot. Thank you.

To my friend Micheline Nader, whom I met at Kripalu during Bruce Lipton's lecture. You shared your book, *The Dolphin's Dance,* and offered help just when I needed encouragement. Knowing you were in my corner kept me going. Thank you!

To my god-sister Lori Carlson Hijuelos, for countless hours talking about writing and publishing. Growing up together at Holy Trinity Lutheran Church, and with your literary background (and your late husband Oscar's Pulitzer-winning legacy), your insights were invaluable. Thank you.

To Maria Kindberg, retired JCC Foundation Director and writing instructor. You reviewed my pile of writing and spotlighted *My Texas Experience* as the first book I was supposed to write. Your encouragement was spot-on. Thank you!

To Chrissy Yocum, who organized my 12 years of scattered files and paperwork. You tackled the chaos on my giant conference table without even reading the book — pure help when I needed it most. Thank you!

To my friend Chris Olsen, Hollywood attorney, producer, and author of *Lucy Comes Home.* Your coaching over the past year has been insightful and steady. Thank you for being such a close ally.

Most importantly, to my wonderful wife, Tammy L. Johnson, thank you for giving me the space to explore myself and my writing, and for standing by me through it all. I love you.

To my boys Colin and Kaden, thank you for being exactly who you are. You've filled our hearts with a love we never knew before. We love you endlessly.

Finally, to my mom and dad, thank you for giving us a loving home where we could grow and thrive. Your unwavering foundation of love and support made all of this possible.

Forward

Greg Peterson

Cofounder, Robert H. Jackson Center

I've spent my career honoring the legacy of Robert H. Jackson — a man who believed in justice, truth, and the courage to stand alone when necessary. But sometimes, the most profound acts of justice happen not in courtrooms, but in quiet moments of reconnection.

In February 2015, over lunch at Shawbucks, I invited Kurt to an interview at the Chautauqua Institution. I thought it might interest him — it was with a doctor whom Mike Wallace had interviewed on *60 Minutes.* What I didn't know was that this meeting would become a turning point in Kurt's life.

Fifteen minutes into the interview, Kurt realized he was sitting across from Dr. Ralph Walton — the psychiatrist he had seen at Jones Hill 30 years earlier. That moment was not coincidence; it was convergence. It was the universe saying, 'It's time to tell your story.'

Lone Star Rising is that story. It is a testament to choosing love over fear, to embracing discomfort as a return to harmony, unity, and oneness.

If you're looking for a book that doesn't just tell a story, but transforms the reader, *Lone Star Rising* is it.

Ralph G. Walton, MD

Distinguished Life Fellow of the American Psychiatric Association

Kurt Johnson's beautiful little book is perfectly timed to help us deal with an era in which machines are capable of deep thinking, utilizing neural networks, and modern physics suggests that quantum potential collapses into physical reality only with observation. *Lone Star Rising* offers a uniquely human perspective replete with profound insight and wisdom. This is not merely a book. It is a living document — a testament to the power of one man's journey to decode the emotional language of the soul. Kurt B. Johnson has crafted a narrative that is both deeply personal and universally applicable. He invites us into his story not as spectators, but as participants in a shared exploration of consciousness.

What struck me most about *Lone Star Rising* is its ability to articulate what so many feel but cannot express. His framework of *Analog Binary Harmetics* offers a new lens through which to view emotional states – not as disorders to be managed, but as signals to be understood.

Having known Kurt personally, I can attest to the authenticity of his voice and the integrity of his message. This book is the culmination of decades of lived experience, distilled into a form that is both accessible and transformative. It is a *beautiful little book,* yes — but it is also a powerful tool for anyone seeking to navigate the complexities of their own inner world.

I am honored to write this foreword, and I encourage the reader to approach these pages not with skepticism but with curiosity and a willingness to let this book be your guide on an ongoing journey toward emotional coherence and spiritual awakening.

Contents

Introduction

"Life is choice, because it's always changing."

- Kurt B. Johnson

This book presents the simple but powerful truth that life comes down to choice. I invite you to join me on my journey as I separate the truth of love from the deception of fear.

I had an experience early in my life where many people wrote me off. The experts said I wouldn't function normally in society. However, not only did I function, I thrived! By realizing that we are all connected — to each other and to everything else — I began experiencing a life free from the bondage of fear-based falsehoods. I embraced the truth that *life is love.* I am just an ordinary man, without advanced degrees or training, who made a simple discovery that allowed me to live a life of harmony and peace.

My goal has become clear: to share this experience and lessons with others, so that they can also thrive regardless of who has written them off or disregarded their abilities. I hope to assist people in escaping the imprisonment resulting from other people's fears and judgments and, more importantly, the self-imprisonment of their own fears and judgments

Inspired by a Question

I am inspired to write this book by a question I asked at age four. I asked a lot of questions at that early age. Not only that, but when I got an answer, I would follow it up with a *Why?* Most children are not afraid to ask such questions. Once we are old enough to begin our schooling, we are encouraged to be obedient and not to question the institutions that try to make us behave a certain way, whether in public or in Sunday school.

Hysterical as he was, the late comedian George Carlin was a fount of wisdom when he said, "Governments don't want a population capable of critical thinking. They want obedient workers, people just smart enough to run the machines and just dumb enough to passively accept their situation."

Our parents and other adults sometimes get irritated, even mad, when we ask *Why?* when they give us an answer. They say, *That's just the way it is,* or they tell us we ask too many questions to stop us from questioning the answers. Sometimes our parents tell us we can't do something, and when we ask *Why?* they give us the meaningless response *Because I said so!*

My dad was a man of honesty and integrity in all things except in his golf game, which was not up to par. He and his buddies played by their own rules, with mulligans, pondies, do-overs, and rolling the ball around for a preferred lie. *If we're having fun and not hurting others, shouldn't we all be allowed to play by our own rules and make our own choices?* He was an only child in a Swedish home and so was used to having things go his way without compromise, but he was not always selfish. He gave willingly to his church every Sunday and enjoyed making others laugh with his great sense of humor. But Dad considered himself head of the house — the ultimate authority. He was not overtly affectionate, yet his sense of humor eased his social awkwardness. He preferred quiet, controlled expressions.

My dad was too much of a macho man to use the word *love,* even with me, his only son. My mother, also raised in a Swedish household, was also not very vocal about her love for me, but she was very kind and hardworking. For some reason, the old-school Swedes don't use the word *love* very often, and they usually try to hide the way they truly feel. She deferred to Dad on almost everything and let him control much of what she did, including how much money she spent. My mom was hearing impaired because of nerve deafness. She mainly read lips. As my mom got older, her hearing continued to deteriorate. Early on, Mom worked as a secretary at a doctor's office until she was unable to answer the phone because of her deafness.

She was an active member of the Thule Lodge — a Swedish club in Jamestown, New York. She was involved in the Swedish dance team and ran the children's club, including the children's dance team. She loved being a waitress there on Friday and Saturday nights. She'd been a member of the Viking Lodge since her teenage years. As was common in her family, she had her bouts with alcoholism, which occurred most strongly from my early childhood through my twenties. These characteristics shaped our family dynamic in ways probably not unfamiliar to many of my age.

My dad would tell me, when I was young, that college probably wasn't an option for me. He would tell me I was more likely headed for the school of hard knocks. I'm not sure if he said this because he couldn't afford to send his second child to college or because he really thought he could see into my future. Either way, I decided to take his words to heart. As the years went by, it became more evident that the school of hard knocks might be my destiny.

My dad also forbade me from having a motorcycle when I was twelve. Many of my friends had motorcycles, and my dad thought they were too dangerous. He was a physical therapist at our local hospital and treated many motorcycle accident victims. I pleaded my case to have a motorcycle. I said, "How about if I pay for the motorcycle myself with my own money?"

He wanted to end the conversation, so he said, "Fine!" If I could save up the money, I could buy myself a motorcycle without his approval. "You could never save that amount of money anyway," he said with complete confidence.

A couple of years went by. I found my dad in his recliner, where he would spend most of his time after work before going to bed. I had spent the previous two years mowing lawns and shoveling snow. I had the money to buy a 1969 Hodaka Ace 100 with a big ol' chrome gas tank. I showed him the $150 I had saved up to purchase the motorcycle. He said, "I never said you could buy a motorcycle."

I called him out and said, "You told me two years ago that if I raised the money for this motorcycle, I could buy it."

He conceded and agreed.

I loved and respected my dad, but that didn't mean we never bumped heads. My dad wasn't the easiest guy to have an open conversation with. When he didn't want to talk about my childhood curiosities, such as the possible existence of Bigfoot or UFOs, he would wrap up the topic quickly by saying, "I doubt it." That meant the end of my questioning.

I knew my dad loved me even though I never heard him say those words until I moved to Texas on a motorcycle at age eighteen. I think it was a Swedish thing, because all my Italian friends' parents and grandparents often told *them I love you.* My dad was a bodybuilder and, as I said, a macho man. Tough guys don't cry, and they don't want to sound weak by saying I love you to their sons.

My parents provided us with a great childhood. I know my mom loved me. She showed it, but she didn't speak the word *love* very often. However, one of her demonstrations of affection prompted a question that inspired this book.

Around December 2012, my mom arrived at my house with my baby book in her hand and a big smirk on her face. She asked me, "Do you remember one of your first questions you asked?"

Of course, I replied, "No."

My mom told me how my pre-K Sunday school teacher had found me crying hysterically in the corner near the kitchen of our church. She attempted to ask me what was wrong, but I was so upset, huffing and puffing, that I couldn't talk or catch my breath. Once she was able to calm me down enough to answer her question, I asked a question of my own:

"Who's Boss Here, Pastor or God?"

Apparently, I was playing with wooden blocks near the kitchen exit door. I wanted to take these wooden blocks outside, and Pastor Bergstrand must've seen me. I'm sure he told me not to bring the wooden toys outside, and that I was only allowed to play with them inside the church. I probably didn't understand why I couldn't play with wooden toys outside. Pastor Bergstrand probably thought they would get damaged. But why was this so upsetting to me? That shouldn't have brought out the tears and made me cry so hard that I couldn't breathe. As a child, I was always full of energy and on the move. My baby book also says I liked to "pound on and fix things." Fittingly, I became a carpenter later in life.

I'm sure my teacher told me that I was in the house of God, and that I should be on my best behavior and play quietly. Church is a place of worship, a place to be at one with God. Perhaps I was more upset about the pastor telling me what I could and couldn't do in the house of God. Who was he to get between my God and me when I'm in God's house?

Pastor Bergstrand and his family were wonderful people. Our church was full of life, fun, and excitement. We even had a youth choir, the Kirk Singers, that would play during our Sunday church services. In the summers, I sometimes wore swim trunks under my shorts because after church, we would head straight to Vikings Lake Park on Chautauqua Lake.

About the age of four, I would jump off the deep end of the dock at the Vikings, and my dad would grab me out of the water. The deep end was over my head. I liked to be brave and impress my dad, plus I had his attention. After a couple of Sundays of this, my dad tried to get me to swim back to the ladder from the safety of his arms. I was scared, afraid to swim back to the ladder. He brought me to the ladder, stepped back, and then asked me to swim to him from the ladder. It worked. I swam alone from the ladder to my father. He taught me how to swim. Soon after, I was able to swim back and forth between the ladder and the safety of my dad's arms.

During our confirmation class, Pastor Bergstrand taught us the New Testament and Jesus's teaching that we are love. "Love your neighbor as yourself." "Do unto others as you would have others do unto you."

"Choose love."

Pastor Bergstrand referred to the Old Testament as "an eye for an eye and a tooth for a tooth" and spoke of God's jealousy. Today, for me, the Old Testament represents control by fear and dying from fear, while the New Testament represents living to love and allowing the discomfort of fear to guide us back toward love.

My first experience with death was my Grandma Doe (Doris), my dad's mother, who passed away when I was around eight years old. She was very fond of me and wanted to spend a lot of time with me before she passed. Part of the reason, I think, is that my dad was born in 1931, during the Depression, and she'd had to work; she wanted to make up for the time she didn't get to spend with my father when he was a little boy.

One day, while I was sitting alone with her on the davenport, she told me she didn't have long to live. It was an emotional, tear-jerking conversation. She wanted me to know that there were two people she wanted me to look up to as role models. The first one, obviously, was Jesus. I should grow up to be like him; he would teach me love. The second one was Honest Abe — Abraham Lincoln.

She gave me a book about Abraham Lincoln's childhood. A hardcover book with red cloth. This book includes stories of Abe growing up with his friend Austin. It also tells the story of how he walked several miles to return six cents to a customer he had accidentally overcharged while working at a general store as a young man. I started reading this book, the first book I ever read cover to cover, after my grandmother had passed. I read slowly; it was painful for me. I would read a page a day because my grandmother asked me to read this book.

I also read the Bible to honor her, but I only read the red print, which represented the words of Jesus himself. I learned a lot about love in these red texts in my Bible, in Jesus's words. I chose love, and pastor Bergstrand reiterated that Jesus's teachings were all about love.

I choose love, and I continue to choose love today.

We are moving out of the Old Testament paradigm of dying from fear and into the New Testament paradigm of living to love. This book is about my journey of learning to choose love over fear and allowing the discomfort of fear to assist us in returning to love.

Life is choice, because it's always changing.

Knowing that you have a choice is the definition of consciousness. I choose love to create positive movement within myself and those around me.

I choose love!

Lone Star Rising

"The Lone Star does not rise from the horizon — it rises from within. When the power of choice aligns with the current of love over fear, we become the charge that lights the world.

We are charged by our choices!"

- Kurt B. Johnson

My Texas Experience

"The only bad experience in life is the one you didn't learn from."

- Kurt B. Johnson

Spring 1984

When my friend Joe Cala suggested I trade in my newly rebuilt 1969 Mercury Cougar for a motorcycle, my mind spun. Trading in my pride and joy was a big ask. I had previously traded a motorcycle, a 1978 Honda CB750K, to my friend Bart Schuver in exchange for that '69 Cougar. I spent my senior year of high school rebuilding the car as a class project for my auto mechanics class. When the car came to me, it had a rebuilt Ford 302 motor and a brand-new Hayes 350-pound clutch. It was built for speed but needed brakes, an alignment, and other basic restoration that I was able to accomplish in and out of the school's auto shop. She spent the winter in my friend's auto body shop getting painted. By the spring of 1984, I was the proud owner of a refurbished 1969 Ford Mercury Cougar XR-7. She was a luxurious, upscale version of the Ford Mustang, featuring hidden headlights. Between her pearly blue paint job and aluminum mag wheels, I felt like she was ready to be featured in *Hot Rod Magazine.* She wasn't perfect, but she was mine, and it was great to see her restoration through to completion.

At about this time, Joe had just bought his first motorcycle, a Honda CB 400 Hawk, and had passed his motorcycle road test. Naturally, he was excited at the idea of taking his new ride out on a long cross-country journey. His first suggestion upon seeing my newly restored car was that I sell it and put the money toward another motorcycle for myself so we could hit the road together.

I thought, *No way.* I had worked so hard on this car and made so many memories. Why would I sell it and downsize to a motorcycle? That seemed foolish.

After some convincing from Joe, I started thinking, *Why not?* The journey sounded like an adventure.

So, I parked my newly redone car in front of my parents' house, put a for-sale sign in the window, listed it in the classifieds of Jamestown's *Post-Journal* newspaper, and sold it to the second person who looked at it. I'm sure I could have asked for more than he offered, but I felt pressured to get a new bike before Joe left without me. Very shortly after, I found the bike of my choice: a Suzuki GS1000G shaft-drive touring bike with a front fairing and a cassette deck.

Now came the hard part. I had to tell my parents about the motorcycle journey Joe and I were planning, and I knew they would not be happy about it. My father, the physical therapist who was not very mechanically inclined, had never been a fan of motorcycles and was adamant that I not own one. "They are a waste of money and dangerous," he would say, as some of his PT work involved the rehabilitation of clients who had been in motorcycle accidents.

As I told my parents of my impending ride with Joe, the look on their faces was one of disbelief and horror. It resurfaced the memory of my accident two years before.

April 1982

A brand-new Holiday Inn hotel, complete with 160 rooms within a seven-story structure, had just opened in Jamestown. My parents decided to book a room for the night to join their friends at the hotel's grand opening celebration. While they were planning their overnight stay downtown, my older sister, who had graduated from high school the previous summer, was in her second semester at Jamestown Community College and was planning a keg party at their house to celebrate.

I was sixteen, a junior in high school, and no stranger to alcohol. I enjoyed hanging out with some of my older schoolmates; this party was a good fit for me. More than a hundred people showed up. Most of them were at least eighteen, the legal drinking age at the time. A group of our friends showed up on motorcycles, and I noticed the guys checking out my recently purchased CB750K.

The guys suggested we take our bikes out to a popular nightclub on Chautauqua Lake called Trader Jack's. Eager to accompany them for a night on the town, I jumped on my bike. I was not fully aware of the dangers of drinking and driving, which wasn't quite as heavily enforced in those days. Mark Norris, a friend of mine who had graduated with my sister, decided to tag along and hopped on the back of my bike. A 215-pound bodybuilder, Mark was significantly larger than I was, with my own 140-pound teenage frame.

As we departed my parents' house, I determined that I was the least experienced biker, so I opted to ride at the rear of the group. We headed out of town on Baker Street, the speed limit increased from 45 to 55, and Mark nudged me as if to say *Keep up!* In my somewhat intoxicated condition, I was happy to oblige. In fact, I did more than that. When the group ahead of me accelerated to the new speed limit, I twisted my grip to full throttle, rapidly shifted gears, and soon left the group behind.

We reached a slight left-hand bend in the road, so I leaned left to follow it. Unfortunately, Mark leaned right, and his weight forced the bike straight. I eased off the gas without downshifting, a BIG mistake, and we coasted over the white line onto the gravel shoulder.

We hit a small snow pile, and we both catapulted over the handlebars. As I flew through the air, time slowed to a crawl. I thought, *Oh well! Here we go!*

Then the chaos — tumbling, rolling end over end across gravel for what felt like forever. I collided with Mark at some point, limbs tangled. All I could think was, *Don't let the bike land on me.* I hoped Mark was okay, but in the blur, I couldn't tell. The world spun, dust and gravel everywhere, and I kept waiting for it to stop.

Finally, it did. I came to rest in front of the motorcycle, wind knocked out of me, gasping for air that wouldn't come. When I stood up, I thought I'd gone blind. The long slide across gravel had shredded my helmet's face shield.

The other riders caught up, and when I flipped the visor open, my vision returned. Mark was walking toward me, battered but moving. Relief flooded through me — this crash could have killed us both.

Another rider, my cousin Bruce, went to the house across the street to call for an ambulance. He also called his brother Dan to get my bike and ride it back to my parents' house.

Mark, with his clothing and brand-new cowboy boots shredded, was in severe pain from impaling the palm of his hand on a rock.

I was a little worse off than Mark. For starters, I was wearing a now-shredded polyester jacket. My blood caused it to adhere to my body, and I looked as if I'd been tarred and feathered. Nothing resembling skin remained on my right arm from the back of my hand all the way up to my shoulder. Hundreds of tiny rocks had embedded themselves in my arm and abdomen, which turned out to be even more painful than my arm during the healing process.

The ambulance took us to the hospital, where the nurses placed us in separate rooms. They discharged Mark about three hours later. I spent the next eight hours, tended to by a nurse, picking the rocks out of my body and removing the dead skin that was still attached to my arm. They couldn't stitch my wounds because I had no skin left to work with. Due to the risk of infection, a skin graft wasn't possible either. My wounds had to remain open for several months to heal properly.

Later, the police officer who'd arrived on the scene measured the distance from the bend in the road to where the bike finally stopped — the length of a football field away. He estimated we'd been speeding well over 100 mph when we lost control. He wrote me a ticket for "Speed Not Prudent."

I am forever grateful to my sister for keeping the news of the incident quiet until my parents could return home from their overnight hotel stay. My injuries were not life-threatening, and I wanted my parents to be able to enjoy their night before finding out what I had done. The following morning, while lying in my bed wrapped in so much gauze that I looked like a bloody mummy, my parents returned. Mom rushed into my room, torn between wanting to beat me for my foolishness and celebrating the fact that I had survived the accident with no permanent damage.

Dad, who had disliked the idea of me on a motorcycle all along, took a more rational approach. He took me on as a patient. We would arrive at his office an hour early for my daily rehab and whirlpool bath. He then would go over my whole body with a pair of tweezers to remove any additional dead skin and check me for infection.

I can imagine the thoughts consuming my parents' minds when I told them about my plan with Joe. After witnessing the aftermath of the horrifying accident their son had so narrowly survived two years before, their now eighteen-year-old son had the gall to say he was trading his car for another death machine! And not only that: the plan was to ride it cross-country with no clear destination in mind and no idea of our return date.

They must have been in a state of shock, as if they'd found out their boy was just drafted into war, waiting for deployment to the front lines. They must have feared that I would never make it home alive, and my accident had not helped them believe I would.

No question, my parents were afraid of the risks, but the road and my adventure were calling. I was eager to meet them both head-on, regardless of any challenges we might face.

The Journey Begins

"Every journey is a circuit. The outgoing path charges you with experience; the return path grounds you in wisdom."

- Kurt B. Johnson

April 1984

Joe and I were greeted by a cold, cloudy day on the morning of our departure. It would be much warmer in Dallas, Texas, which we had now chosen as our destination, but a few hours later, we learned that Mother Nature's plans might override ours at any moment.

I spent the morning packing all the essentials I could fit on my motorcycle, which, thankfully, came with fiberglass saddlebags. We waited to leave until the afternoon, anticipating slightly warmer temperatures, and at one o'clock we loaded up our bikes. I fastened a travel bag and a sleeping bag to my passenger seat. My tent, brought along in case we needed to spend some evenings outdoors, served as my backrest. Lingering in the back of my mind was the feeling of how difficult this day was for my parents. I could see the disappointment on Mom's face as she watched us preparing to leave.

The weather forecast for the next few days indicated snow was on the way, so Joe and I wanted to start heading south quickly to avoid it. If we could get four or five hours of riding in that afternoon, we would make it out of the snow belt.

Unfortunately, in our ignorance, we set out for Erie, Pennsylvania, thinking that it lay south of Jamestown. We spent the first hour of our trip heading due west, and to our dismay, the temperatures dropped as we approached Lake Erie. By the time we reached Interstate 90, it was beginning to snow, and our visibility decreased rapidly as we approached Erie, the epicenter of the snow belt.

Soon, the snow was sticking to the road, making for very slippery conditions, and we had to cut our losses for our own safety. We got off at the next exit and found a Red Roof Inn to stay at for the night, only forty-seven miles and a fifty-minute drive from Jamestown.

The excitement of hitting the road in search of adventure had significantly diminished, a lake-effect snowstorm now essentially holding us hostage in our hotel room. Not so easily defeated, Joe and I decided we would walk from the hotel to Erie's Millcreek Mall, thinking it was only about a mile down the road from us. Walking was something to do, and it would keep us from dwelling too much on our mutual disappointment. After a walk that spanned nearly four times the distance we'd anticipated, we reached the mall and decided to hang out for a few hours. As luck would have it, we came across a familiar face from high school, a friend who graduated high school a year ahead of us, on his way back to Jamestown from college for Easter break.

The warmth of this unanticipated encounter proved to be all too fleeting, as we now faced another four-mile walk back to the hotel. The snow was falling even harder now, and as we were walking, illegally, on the shoulder of I-90, a Pennsylvania state trooper spotted us and pulled over to reprimand us for walking along an interstate highway in low visibility. Thankfully, he was understanding after we explained our situation, and he offered us a ride back to our hotel.

We woke up the next morning at the crossroads of a big decision. It was 9:00 a.m., with the roads still covered in snow, but the accumulation was slowing down. We had to check out of the hotel by 11:00 a.m. and decide whether to continue with our plan to head south or stay put in Erie. The only thing we knew for sure was that turning back, going home with our tails between our legs, was not an option.

Looking back, I have experienced a dilemma like this many times throughout my life — it has played out metaphorically in my relationships, my professional life, my career changes, and even my personal beliefs. It seems that being forced to make big decisions is like that snowstorm that arose seemingly out of thin air. I've come to realize these storms challenge us so we can grow and become stronger, just as bodybuilders must tear their own muscle tissue to rebuild it stronger than before.

Just before checkout, Joe pointed out the visible pavement on the road, in the tire tracks made by passing motorists. We could safely navigate if we kept our wheels nestled within the grooves of those tracks. So we did just that, taking our time and maneuvering slowly to avoid tipping over in traffic. We were fortunate to have other motorists surrounding us, also moving slowly and staying in their lanes. Within a couple of hours, we left those snowy conditions behind us and arrived at our next overnight stop in Cincinnati, Ohio. We spent the next night in Memphis, Tennessee, experiencing our first taste of warm weather. Another six hours brought us close to Dallas. The journey that began with such difficulty took only four days to complete.

When we crossed into Texas, we stopped just shy of Dallas, in Garland, where we knew we could find a cheaper hotel room as we scouted the area for potential employers. The following morning, we made our way toward Dallas and passed a construction site along Interstate 30. By afternoon, we had reached the city proper and were amazed by what we saw. We were, after all, a couple of small-city boys from western New York with little notion of what it was to be in the heart of a major metropolis. Moreover, I felt a sense of familiarity as I recalled the set of the TV drama *Dallas,* which I used to watch with my dad when I was in high school. As Joe and I prepared for bed back in Garland that first night, we made plans to visit the construction site we'd found earlier that day and inquire about job opportunities.

The following morning, we rode our bikes back to the scene and visited one of the on-site trailers. Inside were two men, and Joe introduced us as a couple of New Yorkers looking for work. He asked for $5 an hour, which was about $1.75 above the minimum wage at the time, and to our surprise, we got hired on the spot. We were to report for our first shift the next day. Knowing that we were fresh in town and in need of accommodations, one of the superintendents told us of a newly completed condominium complex with plenty of vacancy. The complex was in Lake Hubbard, about three miles east of the construction site.

We decided to follow up on the super's recommendation and promptly headed to Lake Hubbard, where we met with the woman in charge of leasing the condo units. She was understandably concerned with our young age and lack of funds. She also correctly assumed that neither of us had a history of renting and would therefore have difficulty finding room and board pretty much anywhere. I can only presume an innate motherly instinct must have kicked in because, despite her reservations, she decided to hand us an application and waived the security deposit.

Her kindness didn't end there. When she discovered that we were essentially going to be living out of our hotel room in Garland until something else came through, she promptly handed us keys to one of her condo units. She offered to let us put the money we were planning to spend on our hotel room toward our first month's rent, which she would require from us the next day. The two of us pooled our resources, successfully paid our first month's rent, and signed a lease agreement, grateful for our new landlord's generosity.

We immediately went from being practically homeless to inhabiting a brand-new two-bedroom condo on Lake Hubbard, complete with a built-in fireplace and a community swimming pool. That first night, I went to a convenience store to grab some essentials. As I gathered up some food and supplies and approached the checkout counter, I caught myself staring at the array of cigarette packs behind the cashier, my eyes drawn to the Marlboro Reds. Up until that point, I had never smoked a day in my life, going so far as to make fun of those classmates in my high school who did. I'd thought smoking was both stupid and a waste of money, and I still do, but in that instant, the gravity of my current situation presented itself most unexpectedly. So what if I took up smoking? Nobody knew me in Texas. I came here to start a new life for myself, one in which I could do anything I chose to do without being shamed. I bought my first pack of smokes that night.

Buying a pack of smokes wouldn't be the only first-time encounter of this day. Immediately after checking out, I found a pay phone outside the store and called my parents. My father answered, as was typical, since my mother was almost entirely deaf and had trouble hearing on the phone. I told my dad all the success Joe and I had had during our very brief time in Texas; we'd not only found a place to live but also found employment together, all in the same day! I could hear my dad relaying the news to my mother, who was reading his lips, and she got on the phone to congratulate me, her voice tinged with sadness. It was then that my father picked up the phone again.

"We love you."

The words came quickly, almost hesitantly, but they reached my ears all those miles away. Most importantly, it was my father's voice. Although I knew in my heart that these words he said were true, I became speechless at that moment. It was, to my knowledge, the first time he had ever said them to me. The best I can figure is that seeing his son leave home on a motorcycle for an indeterminate amount of time had pushed my father to his emotional limits. Perhaps, having witnessed the aftermath of a previous motorcycle ride two years before, he thought it was his last chance to tell me so. In either case, hearing those words from my father gave me a sense of accomplishment I'd never felt before. For that reason alone, this journey, although barely begun, had already produced a reward that I would not have dared even dream of. My father loved me. There could be no doubt about it now.

My walk back to the condo that night was pleasant. I relished in my father's words as I smoked my first cigarette. Though I would soon come to earn my now-erstwhile distinction as a smoker, there was something behind my proclivity for Marlboro Reds that would aid me in an entirely unforeseen direction just a few short months down the road.

Summer 1984

All the good fortune I'd found over the previous several weeks made that snowstorm on Lake Erie feel like it had happened a lifetime before. Everything was falling into place. Joe and I had found jobs and a place to lay our heads, and our future in Texas appeared bright.

Though Joe and I lacked prior construction experience, we more than made up for it through hard work and determination. The superintendent at the construction site went so far as to tell us that he was pleased with our performance. Unfortunately, this arrangement proved short-lived. After about a week and a half on the job, the super called us into his office and said the company was overloaded and needed to reorganize its payroll and crews. He promised he would have us back to work in a week or so, if we could manage it.

We went home that evening feeling somewhat deflated, but we quickly set about turning on our phone service at the condo so the super could call us back when our jobs became available again. We also decided to be proactive, in case the construction gig didn't come back around to us. Skimming through the classifieds of the *Dallas Times Herald,* we were amazed at the number of employment opportunities in the greater Dallas area. However, we quickly felt we might be a bit out of our element, as many of the postings listed a minimum of two years' experience in their respective fields. Some listings included titles and descriptions I was entirely unfamiliar with.

What I did understand, though, was dollar amounts. My interest was piqued when I came across an ad suggesting I could earn up to $400 a week. The ad was for a window tint installer at Spectrum Auto Tint in Irving. *I can do that,* I thought. I enjoyed working with cars and perhaps even had an affinity for them, as my experience in my auto mechanics class back in high school taught me. Making the position even more appealing was that prior experience, though preferred, was not necessary for the application process. Even if my two years of auto mechanics class didn't qualify as "experience," there was still a chance I could swing this. I decided to call them first thing in the morning.

At this point, Joe and I admitted to each other that our job search might take us in different directions. When I told him about the Spectrum Auto Tint ad, he showed little interest and said he preferred working in construction to working with cars. I stuck to my decision and called Spectrum the following morning. I spoke with the manager, Kevin, and agreed to make the trip that afternoon to meet with him and fill out an application.

The commute was roughly twenty-five miles and took thirty minutes. As I headed out along Interstate 30 West to Central Expressway North and finally along the LBJ 635 Expressway, I took the opportunity to enjoy another accessory on my motorcycle: the cigarette lighter. With a sense of pride and confidence, I smoked the whole way there.

When I met Kevin for the first time, my anxiety lessened upon noticing a cigarette in his hand. As a new smoker myself, this would contribute to my sense of belonging at Spectrum. Kevin led me down a long, narrow hallway in the back of the showroom to his office. I handed him my application, and he looked it over while we discussed my background and what brought me to Texas. I told him of the decision Joe and I had made to travel the country on our bikes and look for work. As this relatively relaxed interview ended, he asked when I would be available to start and said he would make his decision the next day.

I spent the next day waiting eagerly for the time Kevin had told me to call him. When the clock hit two, I dialed and got the good news: I had the job! It felt like a miracle. That night, I convinced Joe to join me for drinks to celebrate. We learned that Garland — the northeast section of Dallas where we were staying — was a dry area, with no alcohol sales allowed (a small detail which had escaped us when we arrived). So, we rode about twenty minutes outside town on Interstate 30 to the Dolphin Road exit to quench our thirst — a trip we'd end up making many times during our stay.

I had the weekend to celebrate, and I headed out on Monday for my first day at Spectrum. When I showed up for my first shift, Kevin told me to park my bike around the back, where I saw a handful of other bikes owned by my new coworkers. I took this as a sure sign that I would like to work there. Kevin gave me a tour of the building and introduced me to my coworkers. I met with the other installers on staff — Sam, Galen, and Jeff. Sam and Jeff were both from Texas, and Galen was a twenty-one-year-old Iowa native. Galen rode a Kawasaki 1000, and Sam rode a cafe racer. *We're gonna get along just fine, I thought.*

Kevin showed me around the shop and gave me an orientation of the film and tools they used in the window tinting process. He told me I would make at least $200 a week, with increases over time, because the company paid installers by the square foot.

Additionally, I could work as many hours as I wanted and, as I improved my craft, had the potential to take home between $500 and $600 per week. As part of my training, he took me with him to the car dealerships that Spectrum partnered with. We would pick up and deliver the cars to these dealerships that had sold window tint jobs to their buyers. The dealerships we primarily dealt with were Forest Lane Porsche, John Roberts BMW, and the local Chevy and Ford dealers.

There was no doubt in my mind that this was the job for me. Not only was I going to be able to work on these brand-new cars, but I also got to drive them back and forth from the dealerships that sold them. Growing up in Jamestown, I hadn't seen many foreign vehicles aside from Toyotas and Hondas. Now I was behind the wheel of various Porsches, Audis, BMWs, Mercedes-Benzes, and even an occasional Lamborghini.

Galen was in line to be the next store manager at Spectrum, and when he took me under his wing, I was glad for the opportunity. Midway through my first week, he offered to stay late with me one night and do some one-on-one tint work. By about midnight, after about four and a half hours, I had completed my first solo tint job with Galen coaching me the whole way. He said I could bring home $400 a week if I could average two or three cars per day.

Meanwhile, during my first week at Spectrum, Joe had landed a factory job and was making about $5 an hour. He told me he was content with his new work because it offered the potential for wage increases as he learned more on the job. He and I would hit Dolphin Road on the weekends, and after a while, we started becoming comfortable in our surroundings — particularly after a few beers. Neither of us was particularly confident about our ability to approach women at the bars, but we found enough courage in our beer bottles to make the best of it. I couldn't help but notice and be attracted to the Mexican and Puerto Rican ladies in those Texas bars, because there weren't too many of them in Jamestown at that time. Occasionally, we were joined by Galen and Sam, though Sam didn't come out nearly as often because he had a live-in girlfriend. Galen had a roommate, also from Iowa, who had recently married; Galen took every opportunity he could to get out of his roommate's house.

About three months into our Texas stay, Joe had an accident at work. He severed part of his index finger and suffered some damage to a tendon in his arm, rendering it useless. He had to catch a bus back to Jamestown to be seen by his physicians and heal. Things hadn't exactly been panning out as well for him as they had for me. While he was away, I couldn't be sure he would come back to Texas, but I reminded myself that he was always true to his word, and I knew this adventure was still something he wanted to do. I mentioned my concerns to Galen and said that even if Joe decided not to return, I wanted to make something of myself in Texas. Galen suggested we consider becoming roommates, as he sought an escape from his current living arrangement and wanted to give the newlyweds more space.

It was a good deal for me. I had found steady work in Texas, making more than twice what I had hoped for when I started, and the manager had offered to be my roommate. Nevertheless, the decision I had to make was tearing me apart.

Joe returned to Texas about three weeks after he'd left, and we discussed our future together. He said he was going to stick it out for a while, at least until our lease at the condo in Garland ran out in a couple of months. Then he would re-evaluate and figure out where to go from there. He mentioned he wanted to be back in Jamestown for the homecoming of our mutual friend Jim Ross, who was soon to be discharged from the Marines and had introduced me to Joe back in high school.

Jim always had a significant influence on me. Our friendship began when I played Little League baseball. Jim and I went to different elementary schools. I had never met Jim before becoming his teammate. He was the catcher and one of the most respected kids on the team. I always played "left out" (because I sat on the bench for most of our games). I felt shy, insecure, and lost when it came to baseball, but Jim made me feel welcome.

Jim and I became best friends when we went to junior high school together; I was in seventh grade, and he was in eighth. He remembered me from our Little League days and took it upon himself to look out for me in school as a big brother would. He also got me to toughen up a little so I could stand up for myself when necessary. It was Jim who introduced me to many of my best friends in high school. I could talk to him about anything, including religion, and he would always give me the best advice I could get on practically any subject, sometimes even when I didn't know I needed it. He also has the distinction of being the first guy friend to tell me he loved me, beating my own father to the punch.

I was honest with Joe about my intentions, as well. I told him about my opportunity to make something of myself at Spectrum and move in with Galen. It was a bittersweet exchange. Our paths were diverging in Texas. That was where I wanted to be. Joe decided he would stay in Texas until Christmas, then move back to Jamestown and make plans with Jim. He might return to Texas or complete a cross-country journey with Jim, since I had settled in Dallas.

In the meantime, Joe and I had befriended our downstairs neighbor in our condo complex, a divorced single father who had visitation with his son every other weekend. Most importantly, he had a motorcycle and was also friends with a group of guys from Buffalo, New York, located about seventy-five miles north of Jamestown, who were now living nearby. Joe asked our neighbor if he would like a roommate, as I had determined to take Galen up on his offer and move into central Dallas. Our neighbor accepted Joe's offer, and we officially decided to part ways.

A Man on a Mission

"The only source of knowledge is experience."

- Albert Einstein

Looking back on this time, I see a man on a mission. I was unknowingly assuming a self-centered persona like the one I'd seen in my father growing up. I was looking out for number one. I can't help feeling that if I'd known back then what I know now, I would have gone about things much differently.

I shouldn't have left Joe in a lurch like that. He and I had started on this journey together. But when I first tasted freedom and individuality, I became selfish with my money. I could easily have offered to pay a bigger share of our bills, but my parents had raised me to believe money doesn't grow on trees and that you must work hard to save for a rainy day.

My father oversaw all our family's financial matters when I was growing up. He controlled how every dollar got spent; the rest of us, including my mother, had little say. It was his money because he had earned it, and he knew best how to provide for us. My siblings and I had to subsist on an allowance of $1 per week, which we earned through individual chores. My weekly chore was to take the garbage out on garbage day, and if I mowed the lawn, I would get an additional dollar. My mother got a small allowance of $20 a week, but she also earned a bit of tip money from waitressing at the Thule Lodge on Friday and Saturday nights that she could spend on herself.

I now realize how much my father's beliefs and attitudes impacted my own behavior in Texas. My dad was born on February 9, 1931, in the heart of the Great Depression, and I had somehow absorbed his mentality, despite never enduring financial hardship. A thousand miles couldn't separate me from my childhood conditioning. Now, reflecting on the Great Depression, I realize it was essentially a mental construct. There was enough food to go around or plant, enough coal to burn. Still, somehow, we, as a people, bought into the faulty idea that money was everything, even though we had all the resources available to avoid the Great Depression. The Great Depression, in my opinion, was only a mental misconception, just like many headlines before and after it.

No doubt about it, I was learning a lot in Texas. But during all the change that was occurring, I'd yet to see the forest for the trees.

Fall 1984

By the end of summer, Galen and I had moved into central Dallas together. The lease was held solely by him because the complex we were staying in had a minimum age requirement of twenty-one. I was still a nineteen-year-old kid who could have passed for a fifteen-year-old.

We rode to work together every morning, positioning our bikes side by side so we nearly looked like the characters from the TV sitcom *Chips*. Over time, we grew to anticipate each other's maneuvers, be they lane changes or turns, and developed our own system of signals through revving our engines in specific ways to alert each other. On colder or rainier days, we would take Galen's full-sized black Chevy Blazer truck. In my six months of driving to and from work at Spectrum Auto Tint, I experienced all kinds of weather — including hailstorms that required me to take shelter under an overpass. On those mornings when the weather was less than cooperative, it was nice to know that I had the option of an enclosed, four-wheeled method of transportation.

When November came around, I got a call from Joe telling me he was planning to head back to Jamestown for the winter. It was getting colder, and therefore harder for him to commute on his bike. He also mentioned getting into a fight and that it might be best for him to head out for a while until things cooled off. Furthermore, Jim would be back home in April, and Joe said he wanted to ride back down to Texas with Jim to visit me in May or June.

Knowing Joe was preparing to head home, I began thinking more about my friends and family back in Jamestown. I decided to make a short trip and visit them for a couple of weeks during the Christmas holiday. Galen told me it would be no issue to take the time off from Spectrum since business was typically slower during the holidays. I bought my plane tickets and arranged for someone to pick me up at the Buffalo airport.

In the meantime, I set about making some changes to my appearance. I wanted to give the impression to my people back home that I had matured and become successful during the past several months in Texas. I bought a pair of copper-brown lizard-skin boots like the ones Galen wore. They were $250, which was a lot of money to spend on boots — especially back then. I paired those boots with a Texas-style sport coat jacket. I also tried a new hairstyle, forgoing my mullet for a shorter cut that I parted on the side.

I achieved the new look I was going for, but struggled internally to embrace this new persona. I knew I was still the same shy, introverted kid who had left Jamestown in a snowstorm just nine months before and felt like I wasn't fooling anyone with my new aesthetic. Just before Christmas, Galen drove me to the Dallas Fort Worth airport, and I was on my way.

I spent the next two weeks reconnecting with everyone I'd left behind back in April. I went out barhopping with my friends, which was now legal. The previous year, when I had turned eighteen, the drinking age in New York state had gone up to nineteen, and I had had to use a friend's ID to get into the bars. The drinking age in Texas was also nineteen, and so, with my new Texas-issued photo ID, I was good to go. I got the feeling that my friends at home weren't too keen on my new hairstyle, and in all honesty, I wasn't particularly enjoying the look myself. I did get several compliments on my lizard-skin boots, though, because they were a rare sight in Jamestown.

My visit home passed quickly, and soon I found myself back with my new friends and my new home in Texas. Galen and I talked about my vacation and how things had been going at Spectrum in my absence. He also informed me that he had begun dating the Spectrum secretary, Michael Ann. He said she had spent the past week or so at our apartment, and he was considering asking her to move in with us. I heartily consented as his friend, knowing full well this probably meant I was losing my wingman. Michael Ann moved in soon after. Thankfully, everyone got along well at home and at work.

Unfortunately, because business had been slow at Spectrum during the holidays, many employees found time to complain. That made sense — their pay depended on output. Like most installers, they earned money by the square footage of windows they tinted. I returned to a much lower morale than before I'd left a few weeks earlier. Predominant among the complaints I heard was that a new executive recently hired by the owner was aiming to expand the business's commercial tinting of building and house windows. He said there was more money in commercial properties, but the employees thought the shop was making that switch only to be downsized or sold soon. They were also upset that the owner's wife was getting a paycheck even though she didn't work there.

At about this time, Bob, one of the Buffalo natives Joe and I had met through our condo neighbor in Garland, approached me with a business proposal. He asked if I had any interest in owning my own auto tint shop and offered to be a silent partner. He said his girlfriend could finance the operation, and he could assist in running the office. I mentioned to him that the timing of all this was favorable, given the drama at Spectrum. In fact, I was comfortable with the idea of running my own shop, as I'd previously drawn up a hypothetical business model and shop blueprints as part of a project in my high school auto mechanics class. Unofficial as it all had been, I felt I should be able to apply this knowledge to a new venture with Bob.

Adding to my desire to branch out on my own were the rumblings I'd heard among my other coworkers that they were of a mind to do the same thing. The rationale was that Spectrum would get along just fine in the commercial business anyway, since that's where they felt the money was going to be. Regardless, I stayed on with Spectrum until all the other logistics could come together for Bob and me. Given the impact of a chance meeting that occurred within this overlap, I'm glad that I waited.

You've Got It Made in the Shade!

"A penny saved is a penny wasted. Give freely, and life will give back to you in abundance."

- Kurt B. Johnson

One afternoon, Spectrum Auto Tint asked if one of us would be willing to tint a fifth-wheel pickup truck with a driver still inside due to a disability. My arm went up quickly because I had experience working with people with disabilities, thanks to the summers I spent helping my cousin at a Christian home for the handicapped in Wisconsin.

The customer pulled his truck around, and I guided him to my workspace. He opened his door, greeting me with a big hello and an even bigger smile. He appeared to be of retirement age. I was smoking a cigarette, and he noted it was a Marlboro Red. He asked if he could join me, and I consented. We started talking, and he told me his wife disapproved of his smoking. She'd been pressuring him to quit, as a matter of fact. The man had a very genuine personality and seemed interested in me. He asked about my job — how long I'd been working at Spectrum, why I chose to go into the profession — as I went about my work taping his windows before undertaking the tinting process. He also noticed my accent, or rather, that I lacked the Texas drawl. I told him the story of my southbound motorcycle journey with Joe, and he commented on our bravery and courage for leaving home at such a young age.

Eventually, the conversation drifted to the politics behind everything at Spectrum and how a bunch of guys were considering branching off. I mentioned my intention to go into business with Bob, but the man told me bluntly that if I go into business, I should do it on my own or not at all. He said business partners can be difficult, especially when only one of them knows the trade and would be performing all the labor. He also recommended I do this sooner rather than later, as I had youth on my side.

He and I worked through a few different case scenarios as to how this new venture could play out for me, both with a partner and as a solo venture. He asked if I had come up with a name for the business yet, and I told him my idea was to go with Advanced Auto Tint. I reasoned that the name would show up at the very beginning of the phone book's yellow pages.

He then asked about a slogan, but I hadn't thought of one yet. He offered to lend some assistance on that aspect, as his background was in the advertising business for TV and radio. Finally, he introduced himself as Wed Howard. Wed was best known for his radio show, *Melody Magazine,* which aired for nine years starting in the 1950s, designed as a sort of on-air magazine rounded out with music and conversation. He was also the announcer on several network TV shows, including *The Ed Sullivan Show, What's My Line,* and *The Dinah Shore Show.* Wed was said to have been among the first Marlboro Men — hence his interest in my Marlboro cigarette.

As I was finishing up work on his truck, he vowed to come up with a slogan for my new business. He gave me his name, address, and phone number and told me to call him the following week to arrange a meeting.

I called as promised and headed over to his house shortly after. When I pulled up, he was sitting on the patio between his garage and house. He asked for one of my Marlboro Reds, which was fitting, since the cigarettes had jump-started our conversation the week before. His wife came out to invite me in and, though she seemed pleased to meet me, I could see the disappointment on her face at Wed's activities. He mentioned he was not smoking indoors and had cut down to five or ten cigarettes a day — an improvement, as far as his wife was concerned.

As we headed inside, Wed announced that he had a slogan ready. Then he assumed his deep delivery voice and said, "You've got it made in the shade with Advanced Auto Tint." I was instantly in love with this slogan and could feel the idea of a new business venture moving quickly toward reality. *What a catch-phrase!* I thought. I could already see dollar signs.

I followed Wed into the den, his pictures and awards adorning the walls, including many of the famous rock stars from *The Ed Sullivan Show* of the '60s and '70s. It was a very cozy room. His wife brought us some drinks and left us to discuss our business. After a while, she also brought us lunch. We spent a couple of hours together talking about business and life, and he shared his many years of wisdom with me. He told me that Chicago is a great place to live and raise a family. He had a private pilot's license, so he could fly to New York City or California and be home the same night to be there for his family. I was excited because I always wanted to be a pilot as a kid. Wed told so many remarkable stories. It was an extraordinary meeting. I couldn't have met a better mentor, who quickly became a close friend.

March 1985

Reflecting on all my conversations with Wed, I knew that this was undoubtedly the right time for me to set out on my new journey as a business owner. Galen felt the same way when I told him my decision. He figured he'd gone as far as he was going to go at Spectrum. I told him that my grandpa had set aside $10,000 for me, either as a college fund or to help me get started in life. I offered to put up the money to start the business and bring Galen in as a full partner once the company's income had recovered those start-up costs. I needed Galen not only for his managerial skills but also for the side benefit his truck offered. Plus, riding our motorcycles to and from work together was so much fun.

We were confident and ready to get started. We decided to open in April because that was the month that kicked off the busy season for auto sales and window tinting. I quickly procured a business license and insurance, and I leased a section of a newly built warehouse facing Interstate 635 so passing motorists could see our storefront. This location was Bob Beckman's suggestion, who was understanding of my decision to go out on my own but also convinced I was too young and would have a difficult time finding success, at least in the short term.

I was out to prove him wrong by being thorough. I designed my own business cards that featured a small map on the reverse so customers could find us. I also designed price sheets for my walk-in customers and the car dealerships I would be working with.

I called Wed to let him know my decision and that I had signed a lease agreement beginning April 1, with the hope of opening to the public before May. Wed was very enthusiastic about my decision. So excited, in fact, that he wanted to be my first customer. He said he wanted to get all the windows in his fifth-wheel trailer tinted. He offered us the job of tinting the windows at his house, and that would give us extra money to help get the business off the ground. Besides, Wed and his wife were preparing to head up north to Washington State to visit family; the summers in Texas were harsh on his multiple sclerosis. We took Wed up on his generous offer; I am forever grateful to this man for his kindness!

Galen and I grabbed a couple of the other installers at Spectrum to assist us with tinting Wed's fifth-wheel camper. He greeted us all at his house and had two chairs set in front of the camper. When Wed shook my hand, he said, "These chairs are for us. You're the business owner now. These guys are gonna tint the windows for us, and I'm going to school you on business and give you my best bullet points for advertising and marketing."

Once the guys got started on Wed's camper, he shared some key information that I still use to this day. He told me clearly that there are three things that people want to feel, and that I should include them in my advertisements, whether they make sense to me or not. "Include these three things," he said, "and you will run not only a successful advertisement campaign, but also a successful life."

The three things people want to feel:

People want to feel safe.

People want to look and feel good.

People want to feel protected.

"You must address all three of these feelings, and you will draw all the customers you need," Wed said. "Then you must give them the best version of the product that you advertised. It's up to you to build your reputation by word-of-mouth, with good workmanship."

Wed also shared that his career truly took off once he began tithing 10% of his earnings — not just to the church, but to any worthy cause. He firmly believed in giving freely, without attachment. By letting go of the fear of lack, he discovered that money flowed more easily: the more he gave, the more it returned, as if the universe rewarded an open hand over a clenched fist. Those three core human desires he described — to feel safe, good, and protected — applied just as much to money as anything else in life. Hold tight out of scarcity, and you block the current. Release with trust, and abundance circulates. Wed gave me more wisdom than I realized at the time — lessons in generosity that still echo today.

By April 1, the date my lease contract began, Galen, his old roommate from Iowa, and I had painted the walls and floors of our warehouse area — Advanced Auto Tint was open for business! We were lucky that our landlord offered to provide us with the materials if we supplied the labor. Sweetening the deal, he also let us work our first two months rent-free so we could get our feet under us. Since Galen and I had broken off from Spectrum on mostly respectable terms, they contracted with us to send their overflow work, and it was a mutually beneficial relationship. It allowed us to hit the ground running and took some of the pressure off Spectrum, since our departure had left them shorthanded on installers.

When May came around, I heard from Joe and Jim back in Jamestown. They were planning to come down and visit me in Texas. They asked if they could stay with Galen and me while they looked around for jobs. It was great being able to reconnect with the guys, especially Jim, whom I hadn't seen for a long time. I hooked them up with about four days' worth of work with one of my landlord's contractors. Jim had some construction experience from his time with the Marines.

It soon became apparent, though, that neither Joe nor Jim was thrilled in their new environment. I don't think they enjoyed the hustle and bustle of big city life, and they said things felt "plastic" and inauthentic to them. In all honesty, I couldn't entirely disagree with them. A part of me also shared the burden of the big city.

Jim tried to talk me into selling the business and heading to California with him and Joe. Joe was still eager to finish that cross-country ride that he and I had started the year before. Though my conscience, based on experience, told me Jim knew what was best for me, I was still resistant to just picking up and leaving. It was going to be difficult to move; I was starting a business and determined to become financially successful. Working around cars again, I had fallen in love with Porsche 928s, and I wanted to own one.

By June, Joe and Jim had already left, and Galen and I had hired two new employees. The pair had worked part-time at Spectrum the summer before, during their college break. We were seeing a slight increase in walk-in traffic, a sign that the ad I had designed for publication in the *Dallas Times Herald* had been effective. We were also handling many of the major car dealerships in the area, so everything was falling into place.

In July, one of my employees came to my office to tell me that a customer was out front and had asked to speak with the owner. Naturally, I assumed the customer was dissatisfied with the tint job we had done on his car, so I went in prepared for a dispute. Fortunately, the complete opposite occurred — and in the best way.

The man I greeted asked about my age and experience with window tinting and advertising. I told him I was twenty and that I'd been in the window tinting business for more than a year, and I recounted the story of my interactions with Wed Howard. He explained that he was in the marketing business and had selected Advanced Auto Tint after calling five of our competitors and us. He said our newspaper ad was the best he could find in the paper, and that I'd given the best sales pitch to him when we spoke over the phone. Additionally, he was in love with our slogan (thanks, Wed!) and said we more than delivered on our promise.

The businessman went on to tell me he had offices in Fort Worth, New York City, and California. He had been the head of the marketing team that developed the old Rolaids slogan: "How do you spell relief? R-O-L-A-I-D-S!" He mentioned that even without a college degree, a career in advertising wasn't outside the realm of possibility for me. He told me to give him a call if the tinting business didn't work out. This chance encounter had me walking on air. He had delivered a major compliment, leaving me feeling destined for success.

A Night With the Stars

"And as a hero continues the journey, destiny unfolds on Earth while the story is written in the stars."

- Kurt B. Johnson

Though Galen and I were off on our own, Michael Ann was still working at Spectrum and routing some overflow jobs our way. They promoted her from secretary to commercial sales, and a new hire, Elaine, took her place. Michael Ann and Elaine got along well and started getting together outside work with Galen and Elaine's husband, Ron.

Occasionally, I would meet up with this group of friends, but during this time, I often kept to myself in my bedroom while the others watched TV in the living room. I sometimes felt like a third wheel, or in some cases, a fifth wheel, so I decided to give them some space. Also, I was spending a lot of time reading my Bible and trying to understand God's purpose for my life. In this period of reflection, I recalled my religious upbringing throughout school, church, and confirmation class.

In my junior year of high school, I had spent about six months in deep dedication to Biblical teachings. Now, in my quiet time in my room, I was again questioning how I was supposed to love a God I was also supposed to fear. I spent several days contemplating this.

Then one night, drunk and desperate, I stumbled home and asked God for a straight answer. I opened my Bible at random, landing on John 3:16, which begins, "For God so loved the world..." and the truth hit me like a wave. In an instant, I was flooded, engulfed from the inside out, by the pure, roaring energy of God's love. In that moment, I understood: any trace of fear in me dims that love, shrinks it, holds it back. So, I looked up and said it out loud: "God, I choose to love You, not fear You. If You want to send me into eternal damnation for loving You instead of fearing You, then so be it!"

That night, I found one of the bedrock truths I've lived by ever since: fear is the only thing that ever separates us from love, and yet the discomfort fear creates is what finally drives us back to love.

After I came to this realization, I began to understand the purpose of my life: to choose more love and less fear. Most of the time, this is easier said than done, especially for a twenty-year-old kid trying to find his footing halfway across the country from where he started. To this day, I am still on a journey of discovery, embracing the freedom to choose love and move beyond the bondage of fear.

Swallowing Courage

In the mid-eighties, there was a "happy pill" making the rounds, primarily in the bar and dance club circuits. People showed up early to the clubs to purchase one or more of these pills because the supplies would frequently run out. This pill, MDMA, became known as ecstasy; it is an amphetamine-based synthetic drug that produces euphoric and hallucinatory effects for a period of a few hours.

On weekends, I would go out solo to the nightclubs, hoping to make friends and meet a girl to date. I was somewhat shy, afraid I wouldn't know what to say if a conversation arose with someone I didn't know. It was tough to get a conversation going without getting an introduction from someone else. One night, a girl came up to me and asked me why I never asked anyone to dance. I mentioned I was shy and wasn't sure if I was any good at dancing. She said I should try ecstasy. It would help with my shyness, she said, and it was legal. She went on to say it made her feel free, and that she wasn't as concerned with what other people thought of her. "Everything feels free and easy," she said. "I can talk to anyone; I think I can even dance better."

One of her guy friends told me it was a money-saver because he felt so good on ecstasy, he didn't want to ruin the experience with alcohol. He did say, however, that water would become my best friend if I were to ever participate in the experience. "You don't get hangovers, but you will be tired the next day because it makes you go strong for four to six hours," he said.

Ultimately, I decided to give ecstasy a try for myself. The first time I took a pill, I experienced what I can best describe as "an absence of fear." I danced like nobody was watching. No girl was unapproachable, as far as I was concerned. My typical shyness and fear of embarrassment vanished. I was bubbling over with happiness, joy, and newfound freedom. I estimate I took ecstasy four or five times, including once on a camping trip with some friends.

My final experiment took place at our condo complex in central Dallas. My roommate, Galen, had invited our friends to an outdoor music festival. We all popped our ecstasy, drank, and partied until day became night, dancing to all the different bands in a state of perpetual happiness. Back home, after everyone left, I couldn't get to sleep. I was "tapped in" and still turned on, without fear. I said to God that if I could stay feeling this way every day, without having to take ecstasy, my life would be perfect. I was in such a state of enjoyment and at peace, with the absence of fear, that I stayed awake all night.

The next night, I was up wide awake again without the ecstasy, just as I had asked. I was still feeling good, connected, and at peace with the absence of fear. The third night, around 3:00 a.m., I walked outside and looked up into the night sky filled with so many stars. I decided to throw on my swim trunks and go to the pool at our condo.

I sat down on the edge of the deep end with my feet dangling in the water. The water was warm, the air slightly cooler, and the night's silence and tranquility encouraged me to contemplate love and fear once again. Out of the stillness of the night, a single star caught my attention. It took me back to high school and had me thinking about how my fear of difficult dives had kept me from succeeding as a diver.

Taking a Dive

I started diving for the YMCA at the age of seven. When I was ten years old, they canceled the diving program because the deep end of the pool was too shallow, so I switched to swimming. The following summer, I swam for the Greater Jamestown Swimming Team under Coach Rollinger. Before practice one day, I was diving off the springboard, and that impressed Coach Rollinger. I told him of my love for diving and how the YMCA canceled the diving team. He made me an offer I couldn't refuse: I could start practicing with the high school diving team even though I was still in grade school.

I did my best to show off, doing the more difficult dives and trying to be a daredevil. Coach was nervous about this. He told me I should practice the required dives for now and work on my approach so that, when I got older, I could get enough height to do the difficult dives.

Three years later, in ninth grade, I was old enough to dive on the high school team. I had practiced the required dives to perfection: a forward dive, a back dive, an inward dive, a reverse dive, and a twisting dive, along with a forward one-and-a-half somersault in the pike position. I could spring higher off the board than the other divers. I don't remember ever losing a diving competition.

There was one problem: I became afraid of the difficult dives. I had become so comfortable doing the required dives that the discomfort from trying something different overwhelmed me. I never went to the sectionals or the New York state championships because I didn't have enough dives to compete.

Love and fear have played out in so many ways throughout my life. I loved diving, yet I feared difficult dives. From the age of seven, my dream was to be an Olympic diver. In tenth grade, the diving coach at Cornell University basically offered me a scholarship and told me he could help me overcome my fear of difficult dives by moving to Cornell and living with him for my junior and senior years of high school. He assured me he would help me with my studies as well, because I wasn't a good enough student for college at the time. He felt I might be good enough to go to the Olympics if that's what I wanted to do.

I decided not to leave my friends and family, and I didn't believe I could overcome my fear of the difficult dives.

My dad tried taking me to a hypnotist to see if he could remove the mental block that was holding me back from doing these difficult dives. Around the same time, Coach Rollinger introduced meditation into our swim team's practices. He worked on everybody's mindset, not just the physical workouts in the pool, but also the mental workouts. We focused on visualizing how we would perform before the competition began.

One of the former swimmers on the team who was attending college came home to visit on break. He knew me from the time I was in eighth grade and was aware of my mental block. He had been learning the power of hypnosis in college and offered to try it on me. He said these sessions might help me overcome this mental block and remove my fear of attempting difficult dives.

I accompanied him to his brother's apartment, where he gave me the following mantra to repeat: *I can, I will, I shall.* He lit a candle and told me to focus on the flame while he talked me into a hypnotic state. It didn't work because the flame was flickering too much, so he took the lampshade off a lamp in the room and told me to focus on the light bulb. This time, he was able to talk me into hypnosis.

Eventually, these sessions helped me find the courage to try one of the dives I had been unwilling to attempt: an inward one-and-a-half somersault. I successfully pulled it off, but I still wasn't cured of my fear of trying a reverse one-and-a-half somersault or a forward two-and-a-half somersault — both of which I was capable of learning.

Though this experience with hypnotic meditation wasn't entirely effective, I still learned some valuable techniques that I was able to apply later in life.

Sleep Deprived, Awake Forever

As the star in the sky still held my attention that summer night in Dallas, I wondered what would happen if I did a hypnotic meditation on that pinpoint of light, as I had learned in tenth grade. I focused my gaze on that one central point: a single bright star. At that moment, that pinpoint of light held a deep kind of intelligence for me. I allowed myself to lapse into a hypnotic state as I looked up into the night. I reflected on the question I had raised a few weeks prior: How am I supposed to love a God that I'm also supposed to fear? I had chosen to love God and not fear Him. I chose love over fear, even if I would face eternal damnation for not fearing Him.

During all this, with my gaze still fixed on that shining star, I thought of my mom shaming me for not finding a church in Dallas to attend. I contemplated this, then thought of those who go to church out of shame or concern about what others would think if they did not. I realized that others go to church solely out of such fears, and the fear of facing eternal damnation. On the other hand, I also realized that some really do go to church out of love, to give it and to receive it.

In this moment of understanding, a vision came to me, illustrating these two powerful energies in a new way — like a battery with two poles. The positive pole symbolized love, and the negative pole symbolized fear. The image arose from my background in auto mechanics, but the message was altogether simple: We motivate ourselves and others through love and/or fear.

This image prompted me to reconsider what motivates people to go to church, and I realized I couldn't judge that motivation; they were acting out of fear or out of love, embodying one pole of the battery or the other. Perhaps love and fear are at the heart of everything we do. And the choice, to act out of fear or out of love, can have grave consequences. Fear separates us from love, and when the distance between the two becomes too great — when we allow fear to move us too far from love — we suffer trauma, disease, discomfort. But could that fear also eventually return us to love? I hoped so.

This contemplation is my first and most important lesson in human behavior, and it is the driving force behind what I have grown to call *Experiential Philosophy.*

I began to recognize how these invisible forces of love and fear create movement and influence our physical lives, our reality, and our decision-making. I remembered the three things people want to feel that I learned from my mentor, Wed Howard: people want to feel and look good, feel safe, and feel protected. These are all positive feelings.

And then it hit me: our words carry a positive or negative charge. Our words may precede our feelings. Biblically, John 1:1 states, "In the beginning was the Word, and the Word was with God, and the Word was God." Is this how creation works? Are we creating positive or negative experiences based on our words, thoughts, and feelings? The contemplation of this possibility sent me even higher. This understanding continued to evolve over the next forty years, culminating in my own Experiential Philosophy. This philosophy continues to support me in overcoming obstacles and setbacks to this day.

Falling Star, Meteoric Rise

With my eyes focused intently on this bright star in the clear Texas sky, I also concentrated on drawing long and gentle breaths and exhaling even longer.

I allowed myself to sink deeper into this trance-like state, not knowing or even caring where my mind was about to take me. My body was tingling all over; my heart and breath slowed. Yet I felt I had the strong energy of a fast runner flowing through me. I was comfortably energized and tranquil in a deep state of love. It flowed beyond physical feelings of happiness and joy.

I reflected on my recent discovery of fear as a limitation of love, which had occurred to me before I had ever even taken ecstasy. A deep sense of accomplishment engaged with my feelings of happiness and joy. I was learning to understand more deeply how people tend to do things out of love, while others do so out of fear. As before, I envisioned the poles of a battery, with the positive symbolizing love and the negative, fear. I realized that the energies of love and fear both create movement. Shame, guilt, embarrassment, fear, and judgment consumed some, while love, acceptance, and joy guided others. But how could I move people from fear to love? How could I help them understand that the choice was theirs to make? It was, after all, just a choice.

Suddenly, a strange sensation overwhelmed me. I felt as though I had become the eyes behind the eyes of several Eastern and Western religious figureheads — from the greats of the Bible, such as Abraham and Jesus, to the central figures of Buddha and

Mohammed. I knew I wasn't any of them, but inexplicably, I felt like I had parts of them. I know the ecstasy was not in my system anymore to enhance this feeling artificially. The feeling was real at the time, and I still feel it to this day.

I finished my hypnotic meditation, swam, and returned home to my condo. I once again didn't sleep at all that night. Instead, I slipped into what I believe was an egoic-spiritual trip. I had the key to life's mystery, the answer to why we do the things we do. I was also reflecting on the high points of my business, founded on Wed Howard's advice. Between that success and my chance encounter with the advertising rep behind the Rolaids ad slogan, my ego was spiraling out of control, and this bizarre spiritual trip continued into the next day.

For a fourth consecutive night, I got no sleep. I informed Galen that I hadn't slept and told him to go to work without me. I took the day to myself and spent more time swimming and diving in our complex's pool before taking some high-speed motorcycle rides that earned me a speeding ticket. When Galen came home, I tried to tell him about my moment of enlightenment from the night beside the pool, instructing him almost as a teacher would a pupil.

My sleep deprivation stretched into its fifth night, and my egoic-spiritual trip became increasingly chaotic. I had been saying things that were hard for Galen and Michael Ann to understand, things they hadn't thought about before, first thing in the morning. I had the idea that I could leave a trail of notes and objects around the house for them to follow and gain understanding. I wrote some notes and arranged household items, like a light in the kitchen and a cup in the living room. I wanted them to understand who I was and what could happen to the world, but I had to find a way to make them listen. I must have crossed a line when I used my unloaded shotgun and samurai sword as props, because that's when they started talking about getting me some outside help.

Anyone who goes four or more days without sleep will become disharmonious in self, mind, and body, and so Galen and Michael Ann were rightfully concerned about my well-being. They were in a tough position. It was obvious that I needed help, just not the kind of help I was about to receive.

Galen had made friends with an attorney on a kitchen remodel job a few years before. The attorney advised them to get me a doctor's appointment for a diagnosis and to see if hospitalization might be necessary.

Friday, July 26, 1985

I agreed to see a medical doctor to diagnose my inability to sleep. I knew my friends were upset about me using a shotgun as a prop to try to explain my new understanding of fear and love. I figured they were afraid I might harm them or possibly harm myself. Nothing could have been further from the truth. I realized I hadn't been sleeping since the previous weekend, and perhaps seeing a doctor might help me sleep.

As I went in to meet with the doctor, he was aware of my use of ecstasy and showed concerns. He mentioned that my friends were concerned as well. He recommended that I admit myself to the hospital for an evaluation. I didn't have insurance, and I knew a hospital stay would be expensive. I was afraid of losing my business if I went into the hospital. Besides, I just felt that if I got proper sleep, I would be fine.

The doctor was upset that I wouldn't admit myself into the hospital. He prescribed Thorazine in an attempt to help me sleep. He recommended coming back first thing in the morning if the pills didn't help me get some sleep.

I started to believe they were arranging an involuntary hospitalization. I was still unable to sleep Friday night. Some friends spent the night with me to make sure everything was okay. The doctor felt I was suicidal, so maybe that had influenced their decisions. As God is my witness, I never said I was suicidal to anyone, and I wasn't depressed, but maybe my actions with the shotgun misrepresented my intentions.

Once again, I failed to get any sleep that evening, so my friends escorted me back to the medical doctor's office first thing Saturday morning. I had a sense that something wasn't right with what was happening. During my return visit, the doctor insisted there was something wrong with me and that the ecstasy had screwed me up. He told me that I had to go to the hospital. I tried to explain my spiritual awakening of fear and love, and the details of what really happened with my friends. The doctor became irritated with me, calling me delusional and saying that I didn't know what I was talking about. I still felt this wasn't the best care for me, and I certainly didn't believe the best path forward would end at a hospital. I wanted assistance sleeping and figuring things out after a whole night's sleep.

When we got home, everyone decided to spend the day at our place. The doctor said it was vital for me to get some sleep and not to be left alone. I might have slept for a short time.

It was a hot July day. I was wearing white shorts, but no shirt or shoes. Ron and Elaine recognized that I must not have slept much the night before. They convinced me to lie back down and get some more rest. Elaine lay down, too, and cuddled me as a mother would cuddle her little boy to sleep.

In all this sleep deprivation, I must have become more intuitive, because I remember jumping out of bed and saying that I was an important prophet, and they were coming to take me away. Shortly after, a knock came at the door. Six policemen were ready to escort me to the hospital for further evaluation. I wasn't even allowed to put on a shirt and shoes. They cuffed my hands behind my back and off we went.

From Terrell to Hell

"The road to hell is paved with good intentions."

- Traditional Proverb

Just One Night, They Said

My friends said they would meet me at the hospital. Even though I figured it was about two or three in the afternoon when the police came, I must have lost a few hours along the way, because it was almost dark by the time I arrived at Parkland Memorial Hospital. I exited the police car, and the officers walked me down a long, narrow hallway lined on either side with patients sitting in chairs and on the floor. They all looked like they had been on drugs or were drunk. Some of them even looked homeless. I was the only one in handcuffs, though, and still without a shirt and shoes.

Suddenly, one of the patients started jumping up and down. She pointed in my direction and cried, "It's the savior here to save us! I knew he would come!" Unfortunately, this only fed my delusions that I was someone special. I began wondering if I was about to be tortured — or if these people genuinely wanted to hear more about my experience.

We reached the end of the hall and rode an elevator to another floor. Another long hallway stretched out, all doors closed, with a nurse emerging from behind a glass-encased station. She told me my friends were waiting on the other side of the glass. She handed me several forms to fill out, and at last the police officers removed my handcuffs.

I was buzzing with overstimulation — hyper, scattered — and struggled to focus on the paperwork needed before evaluation. When the nurse returned, the forms were still incomplete. She asked one of my friends to help finish them.

Before leaving, she pulled me aside with a quiet warning: Stay away from the woman who kept claiming she was carrying my child through immaculate conception. Back in the 1980s, when the AIDS epidemic was emerging, it was terrifying, mysterious, and poorly understood. The nurse likely worried less about the woman's delusions and more about the risks she might carry, possibly from life on the streets. Her caution came from concern, not judgment.

Ron assisted me in filling out my forms, and then it was time for blood work. However, I wasn't ready to comply. I didn't want anyone sticking needles into my arm. What about that AIDS epidemic I'd just been warned about? Ron took the nurse aside. He returned with their verdict: they needed my blood to study how it worked and hunt for any trace of drugs. I told him they weren't ready to discover what's in my blood; if they found out how it worked, they wouldn't need me anymore and might kill me.

"If you're so in control of your body, let them put the needle in your arm and stop your blood flow; let's see if you can really do that," Ron said. I agreed to this. The nurse wrapped a tourniquet around my bicep and put the needle in, but no blood came out. Ron told me to give her a little blood and then stop the flow again. She stuck the needle back in, got a trickle of blood, and nothing more.

"Let's see if you can fill a vial now," Ron said. In went the needle; I allowed the vial to fill and stopped the flow again. Ron said I would need to fill three more vials before they let me go home. After being stuck about ten times, all the vials were full, and the nurse wrapped my swollen, needle-ravaged arm in gauze.

By this time, the rest of my friends had already left the hospital, leaving only Ron behind to stay with me. The nurse returned a few minutes later and told me I would have to stay overnight. Obviously, in my extreme state of paranoia, I objected to this because I figured that was her way of saying they would be keeping me there indefinitely. She assured me, however, that it was only a one-night stay for observation so they could make sure I got some sleep and give me my blood test results in the morning.

Two muscular security guards entered and stood on either side of me. A feeling of impending doom fell upon me even as the nurse told me I was completely safe and wouldn't be left alone. I said goodbye to Ron, thanking him for his help, and once again thought, *Oh, well, here we go!* The very same thought I'd had as I flew through the air during my motorcycle accident years before. Everything inside me screamed that another crash was just down the road.

The guards took me down the hall, the same one I'd walked down when I arrived with the police. But this time, one of the doors stood open. As we got closer, the bare floor came into view — just a dirty mattress, no sheets, no pillows — and white, burlap-like padding covering every wall.

Once again, I resisted, this time physically. I would rather have spent the night in the reception area than this dingy room. The guards tried to force me into the room, and I fought them as much as I could until one of them said, "Like it or not, you're going in there!" At that point, I gave up, allowing them to shove me into the room. I leaned up against the back wall in resignation, feeling like I was a prisoner despite having done nothing wrong.

For the first few minutes, I prayed and even spoke in tongues, as we did during our high school visits with the Charismatic Christian Movement in Cattaraugus, New York. Suddenly, I felt a sharp pain in my right arm where the nurse had taken my blood. The only source of light in the room, the small window in the door, revealed that the inside of my elbow had swollen to about the size of a baseball. And it seemed to be getting bigger by the moment.

I panicked, yelling for help. But no one came to check on me. Isolated in this small, padded room, I pounded and punched the walls and door. I started to think I was going to die in there and nobody would ever hear my story.

Just then, I noticed a young girl looking through the window, but she was gone as quickly as she had arrived. I called out to her, pounding and punching more to get her attention, and, to my great surprise, she came back. I showed her my arm, and the look of horror on her face did little to soothe my nerves. She ran to the nurse's station, and I heard her pleading my case to the nurse, but to no avail. The nurse still wouldn't see me.

I collapsed onto the floor, completely defeated. In that moment, I was sure the hospital wanted me dead. So I looked up and prayed out loud: "If it's my time, God, come take me. I'm ready." I had no idea what was happening. Until this moment, I'd only ever seen padded rooms in movies, and now I found myself locked inside one.

I felt exhausted, as though a heavy black iron curtain were falling over my eyes. I resisted no longer and, for the first time in five days, submitted to the darkness.

"Your Room is Ready"

Awakened by the hospital staff the following morning, with a security guard present, they told me my room was ready. I groggily accompanied the security guard down some more hallways and onto another elevator ride.

We got off the elevator and went through a security door, and I heard people talking. When we arrived in my room, I found it occupied by around a dozen beds. Still feeling completely exhausted, I immediately dropped down on my bed to begin a twenty-four-hour sleep session.

I woke up again on my third day in the hospital. I heard a group of people talking outside my room, gathered around a TV to watch news coverage of an airliner crash at the Dallas Fort Worth Airport, the Delta Airlines Flight 191 incident of August 2, 1985. After a while, I became familiar with the roughly twenty other patients in my unit. We often sat around the TV watching continued coverage of both the horrific plane crash and the ongoing AIDS epidemic.

I stayed in this part of the hospital for about a week before being relocated to another section for another week. When I finally saw Galen, I learned that he had come to visit the week prior but wasn't allowed in to see me. He told me he'd left a carton of cigarettes, some magazines, some clothes, and gym shoes, though I only recall receiving a single pack of smokes. They never gave me the clothes or my shoes. Instead, they were forcing me to wear those goofy-looking slippers the whole time.

I'm sure this had to be a difficult time for Michael Ann and particularly for Galen, as our business was in my name. He had no access to the checking account that allowed him to pay our bills, our employees, and himself. After it became apparent my hospital stay was going to extend beyond a week, my continued absence put him in a tailspin.

The Van Ride to Hell

One afternoon toward the end of my two-week stay at Parkland Memorial Hospital, the guards escorted the patients in my unit into a waiting room to be seen by the head doctor. I was still under the impression they were trying to figure out who I was and what to do with me. I still believed that I had the gift of some secret, sacred knowledge from above, and that they were searching my blood for answers.

When it was time for my interview, I was skeptical about the reason for this meeting. As the doctor was screening me, one of his eyes appeared larger and more prominent than the other. The larger eye pierced me with a power I didn't feel from the smaller one — likely a false perception on my end. I also believed him to be a Nazi interrogator at the time.

That evening, there was a lot of concern among us patients. We were all scared about potentially being sent to Terrell, Texas, referred to as *hell,* for further evaluation. Another group of patients had been at this screening, as well; younger and more "normal" by comparison. They must have been staying in another unit of the hospital. As I lounged in one of the carpeted circular seats in our commons area, trying to get some rest, a group of three young high school girls brought a children's book over and wanted me to read through it with them. They told me I had to stay awake, or I'd be on my way to Terrell, and they were concerned for my safety.

The next thing I knew, I was crammed into a van with about a dozen other patients. The emotional tension among us was palpable. After we loaded up, a gentleman with a stern, commanding voice warned us not to try escaping, or we'd end up in a straitjacket. He made it very clear that we were to avoid eye contact and speaking with one another. The trip would take about an hour. I assumed the worst: Terrell.

About twenty minutes into the ride, one of the patients toward the back started acting out: kicking at the window, screaming, and flopping around like a fish out of water. Two guards ran over to subdue him. I was afraid of turning around to see what was going on and kept my eyes forward as instructed.

But I heard them beating him, and I'm sure he wound up in a straitjacket. Chaos, confusion, and fear surrounded us. I believe we all felt death lurking.

When we pulled up to the complex in Terrell, my fears were confirmed. Officers escorted us into the building, handcuffs biting into our wrists. They gave us a quick physical — checking our teeth, eyes, and noses — then herded us single-file into the building that would be our new home. They sat us down for a grim orientation, then separated the men and women and took us to our sleeping area, which I estimated could fit about thirty guys. Every other day, we were to undress completely, form a line, and head to the showers. The guards would watch us to make sure we showered. I dreaded these days. It was such a degrading experience.

I felt like I was living in a concentration camp. There was nothing to do and no one to talk to. About a week into my time in Terrell, one of my fellow inmates told me I was being over-medicated because I was sleeping too much. I recall having trouble talking and communicating during this time. He suggested I request cutting back on the number of pills they were giving me. I brought this up with the person who handed me my pills that day. I said I didn't want to take them. Almost instantly, he beat me and tackled me to the ground while a security guard stood there watching it happen. I called out for help and, thankfully, roused a large inmate who looked like a biker and had been sleeping nearby. When the inmate stood up, the beating stopped, and they let me go.

None of this helped my cause. I became a target for the guards, and my medication intake remained the same. I was sleeping about twenty hours every day, and I don't remember being fed by staff because I was sleeping so much. On the days I could get myself up in the morning, I went to the commons area. Oftentimes, I could find this one woman sitting quietly on a couch. She would sit there, staring straight ahead, minding her own business. Many times, I would lie on the couch next to her, put my head in her lap, and drift off to sleep again. She never seemed to mind, and I don't recall speaking with her much at all. Sometimes a man would come and visit this woman. He was bald and looked older. He reminded me of Captain Stubing from the old TV show *Love Boat.* One day, when the man came to visit, she was allowed to leave with him. They were both very emotional at this news, and I was, too. Sad because I would no longer have the comfort and safety I felt when I lay my head on her lap, but happy that she would finally be free of this hellhole.

After the woman left, I spent my days sleeping. I would get out of bed every other day only for mandatory showers and to change my clothes. I often reflected on my happier days, even back to my pre-kindergarten Sunday school class, when we would stand in a circle and sing "This Little Light of Mine." All of us children were always so excited that we were allowed to dance and jump around the room to this tune with abandon, as if nobody were watching. This song gave me hope that "this little light of mine" was God's love within me, and that it would lead me to happier times. These memories kept me going.

The other inmates seldom received many visitors, and I believe we were only allowed them on weekends. After my first week, Galen and Michael Ann came to visit me. Galen looked shaken. He let me know he had contacted my parents, and they were trying to get down to Terrell for a visit the following week. He was closing the business because he couldn't run it without me, and he was running out of money. They were also considering moving to California since his parents had already moved out that way from Iowa.

Mama, I'm Coming Home

"Sometimes, home is not a place — it's a promise. and even when the body is broken, the soul remembers the way."

- Kurt B. Johnson

The following week, my parents made it down to see me. By this time, it felt like everything I did was happening in slow motion. As I walked through the doors into the common space to meet with them, my parents were seated on one of the couches, about thirty feet from the entrance. It felt as though it took me five minutes to close that short distance. Tears ran down my mother's face.

My mother later told me she hardly recognized me at that moment. I was skinny, could barely walk, and was moving and speaking in slow motion. In just over four weeks, I had gone from a healthy 165 pounds down to 111. She said I looked like a prisoner of war living in a prison camp, which was exactly how I felt. I thought I was a prisoner of some secret war, held hostage. I still believe that I may not have made it out of Terrell if it hadn't been for my parents and their efforts to bring me home.

Years later, I came to understand that my father believed he was doing what was best for me by having me institutionalized. He felt I needed to be punished, that I needed to think about what I had done and learn a lesson. And if it took a stint in a mental health facility to do it, so be it. He wanted me to understand that my own actions, my decision to try ecstasy, were the determining factors, that I was responsible for everything that happened as a result. Little did he know how I was barely hanging on.

My release wasn't an easy process, however. Apparently, I was sentenced to ninety days of observation before the *professionals* could evaluate me for potential release. My parents arranged for my release into their custody, on the condition that they would immediately place me back into a mental health hospital upon my return to Jamestown. I could not spend a single night in their house. They were required to admit me to a hospital in New York on the same day as my extradition from Texas, a few days down the road. I would have to fly home with my mother while my father stayed behind to collect my belongings and drive their car and trailer back.

Once again, I felt I had been an embarrassment to my parents. As a physical therapist at Jamestown's WCA Hospital, my dad helped me get into a newer department at Jamestown General Hospital called Jones Hill. If it hadn't been for this, it's likely my parents wouldn't have been able to remove me from Terrell when they did. They might have shipped me straight to a state hospital.

My parents told me they would spend the next few days packing my belongings, closing out my business and personal accounts, and booking the flights to get me home and situated at Jones Hill. In my heavily medicated state, I listened without emotion, feeling disconnected from everything. They were worried about sending me home with my mother on a plane due to her deafness. Because of this, we would need my ears to hear announcements at the airports. They were also concerned about what might happen if I were to become separated or run away from her; they didn't know what I might be capable of.

When the day finally came for my release, I went through the motions. I should have been happy to be out of Terrell and back with my family, but I was so out of touch that I couldn't be excited about anything. They gave my parents a brown envelope containing all my medical records, and my mom and I boarded our plane. True to her word, she admitted me to Jones Hill upon our arrival in Jamestown. Once again, I spent my first night in my new home confined to a padded room. The next day, my good buddies Joey and Jimmy visited me. I had not seen them since their visit to Texas in May. It was far from a happy reunion, though, as I had little to say.

When my parents first met with my doctor, Dr. Walton, he told them I had been simultaneously taking three psychiatric drugs, two of which were Lithium and Thorazine. The doctor commented that my Thorazine dose was somewhere around 1,600 milligrams, which was by far the highest he had seen. Later, my counselor, Mike Connor, shared that my blood work upon admission showed six drugs, despite the paperwork only accounting for three. My parents and the doctors agreed to reduce these medications and their doses as quickly as possible so they could see what they were working with.

There was a suspicion that I might have sustained some permanent brain damage from my ecstasy use. Yet, they were uncertain whether this was truly possible because there had never been a case of an ecstasy overdose in the area. Regardless, the doctors informed my parents that I would need a two-week recovery period. At that time, if deemed I was unable to return home, I would be admitted to a state hospital for another ninety days.

My parents and my friend Jimmy visited every day. Most of my other hometown friends may have been embarrassed to see me because I was certifiably nuts during this time. However, Jimmy came to see me — sometimes twice a day. Still acting the big brother, just as he had in junior high, he stood up for me, even going as far as to confront another patient, older and bigger than I was, who appeared to be bullying me. After Jimmy finished with him, that patient never bothered me again.

During my two-week recovery period, they weaned me off the Lithium because I had never shown any signs of mental illness before. They also reduced my Thorazine dosage, the only medication

I was taking, to 1,200 milligrams. My parents insisted on bringing me home after these two weeks; thankfully, Dr. Walton agreed. He said I was to see a psychotherapist at least twice a week for the first month or two.

I was happy to be home, though my new cigarette habit wasn't going over so well with my parents — especially when I smoked indoors. My younger sister was still attending high school at this point, while my older sister had moved to Florida to live with her boyfriend, whom she would later marry. I had been diagnosed with depression, and my mom had put my name on the prayer chain at her church. I think she was afraid of what the congregation might think if they learned her son may have overdosed on ecstasy.

After a few weeks of becoming reacquainted with living at home, I started going out drinking with my friends again, obviously ill-advised, as my doctor said drinking might adversely impact my medications. He had also informed me that were I to stop my meds cold turkey, my heart could give out, or I could experience a seizure or stroke.

The dangers could not dissuade me from my desire to smoke and drink at will, and so out on the town I went. One night, I remember becoming especially drunk, walking out into the street in front of a bar called the Rusty Nail, and directing traffic at about one o'clock in the morning. Although I'm not entirely sure my parents ever found out about my late-night traffic control job, they were generally horrified and embarrassed by my behavior. I was not behaving like the son they used to know, and they began thinking that perhaps the doctors had cut my medications back too quickly. My dad decided it was time for me to return to Jones Hill because being home was not safe for me.

I, too, had realized something wasn't right, and I came around to thinking that it was likely I had a chemical imbalance brought on by my ecstasy use. I returned to Jones Hill worried about whether they would send me straight to a state hospital. Fortunately,

Dr. Walton told my parents that relapses are normal, though not usually as quick as mine had been. He said he would give me a couple more weeks but told my parents to prepare for the worst. He encouraged them to choose which state hospital they preferred if this period didn't work out.

On one day during this second stay at Jones Hill, I witnessed someone leaving the hospital via a rear-door exit at the end of a hallway. Realizing this was my ticket to freedom, I made a run for it! With an orderly chasing after me, down the back stairwell to the door, I turned around and growled at him. He quickly gave up his pursuit.

I ran downhill, about a quarter mile away from the hospital, toward the Chadakoin River and a bridge to freedom, when I spotted my good friend Mike driving along in his car. He shouted toward me, so I ran up to him, saying that I needed a ride. He asked me where I wanted to go, but I hadn't thought that far ahead. So I told him to take me to the Thule Lodge, the Swedish club my mother frequented almost daily. Mike dropped me off, and I went inside. Everyone there thought I had come to see my mother, but she wasn't there. They called her down to the lodge, and she brought me back to Jones Hill.

Nothing was going according to plan. My parents were angry and concerned that I was going to become a permanent state hospital resident. Dr. Walton offered an alternative treatment option: electroconvulsive therapy. Electroconvulsive therapy involves passing a controlled electrical current through the brain to induce a brief seizure, potentially resetting disrupted neural pathways when severe depression resists all other treatments. Dr. Walton said that if depression were indeed the root of my problems, this therapy would likely help, but it was a last resort. He had seen it work in similar cases. Feeling cornered with no better options, my parents consented on my behalf.

I have no memory of anyone explaining the treatment to me. I only remember staff directing me to sleep in the padded room beside the nurses' station with the door left open. I was awoken the next morning by three orderlies and given a shot. I believe they put me through two ECT sessions, but I have no memory of them.

It took my mother a whole year to confess what they had agreed to. The guilt weighed on her heavily. When she finally told me, I was angry at first — feeling betrayed by a system that treated me more like a problem to fix than a person with a voice. But over time, I came to a different understanding. Those sessions sped my release, kept me out of long-term state care, and brought me home sooner. In the fear-driven world of medicine back then, it felt like the only path forward — even though I had lost all trust in our health care system.

They allowed me to go home again after ECT, but I was still not quite out of the woods. I was still taking about 1,200 milligrams of Thorazine, which caused me to sleep a lot, and I was now starting up my psychotherapy sessions with Mike Connor, who also worked at Jones Hill. Mr. Connor gave me some critical advice early on. He realized I was homebound until the doctors could reduce my medications enough for me to function at a job. He told me to take my time getting to know myself and what I wanted to do and be in life. He wanted me to consider this seriously because it was an opportunity not everyone gets — taking the time to assess these things before committing to a full-time job or a family.

After about four months of these sessions with Mr. Connor and a psychiatrist from Buffalo, Dr. Gorman, I was contemplating what kind of work I might pursue. The question remained as to whether I might have sustained brain damage, and, if so, to what extent. The doctors recommended an IQ evaluation. My mother took me to the test, and the following week, I visited Mr. Connor' office to get the results. He warned me that the high doses of Thorazine I was still taking might skew the results. I scored well in math but at a third-grade level in reading. My score was very low, around 65. This score indicated a severe intellectual disability. My mother was devastated by this news, fighting back tears because she didn't want me to lose hope.

Mr. Connor suggested I eventually look for work at The Resource Center in Jamestown, which served people with developmental disabilities. They had a wood shop there that could be a good fit for my particular skill set. He also recommended that we wait to apply until they could scale back my medications even further.

I was devastated by the results of my IQ test — especially the one that set my reading level at third grade. Growing up, reading had never been something I enjoyed or prioritized. I could read well enough to get by — faking my way through assignments early on, discovering CliffsNotes in junior high, paying close attention in class, and taking good notes. I assumed that I was functioning at a minimum of a tenth-grade level.

But the truth was, I avoided reading whenever I could. It bored me, frustrated me, and felt like a chore — not because I couldn't do it, but because I wasn't interested. Schoolbooks didn't grab me, so I chose other things instead. Learning I was years behind crushed me. It felt hopeless, like I'd never amount to anything or build the future I wanted.

When I confided in Jimmy, he said it was because of the medications I was taking. He said there was nothing wrong with me and I should get off all of them right away, regardless of what the doctors said. I explained the warnings I had received about stopping them abruptly, and, even if I didn't die from heart failure or a stroke, my father had also said he would personally admit me to the state hospital if I stopped. This possibility terrified me. There was a lot at stake if I took Jimmy's advice. I couldn't stop thinking about my time in hell, back at Terrell, and wondered if all state hospitals were like that. Could I afford to take this chance?

Spring 1986

One day in March, Jimmy came over on his Kawasaki 900. The weather was still cold, maybe fifties at best. I was home on the couch, alternating between watching TV and sleeping, as usual. Jimmy said I should get my bike registered, insured, and back on the road because it would give me something to do.

At the time, I didn't feel I was coherent enough to operate a motorcycle anymore, but Jimmy didn't see me that way. I also didn't feel like I should be going out and having fun before I could land a steady job, and I wasn't so sure my parents would go for it, either. However, I still had money from my business in Texas, so I put my bike back on the road.

By April, the doctors scaled back my meds even more. On the warmer days, Jimmy would come by, and we'd go for rides together. By the end of the month, I was offered a job at JNK Machine, the family business of one of my friends, Bart Schuver. They primarily dealt in repairs and replacement parts for semis and tractor-trailers. They also sold heavy springs and snow plows.

It was difficult for me to get up in the mornings, and I often felt like I was waking up with a hangover. At work, I had difficulty remembering what I was doing and how to find the inventory I was looking for. At home, I couldn't even remember all the steps to taking a shower — the soap, shampoo, and towel. My time at JNK lasted only a couple of weeks. I felt like I was costing his business more money than I was worth, and I didn't want to be a charity case.

In May, Jimmy received some terrible health news. He had been suffering from headaches and thought maybe they were due to his eyes. After having an examination, he learned that he had low blood pressure in his eyes. He was sent to the hospital for further examination and was diagnosed with leukemia very shortly afterward. Jimmy was the first friend I'd known to receive such a devastating diagnosis. I was worried for him because everyone I'd known from church who had cancer had died from it.

Jimmy went to Roswell Park in Buffalo to start his chemotherapy sessions. We still found time to take some motorcycle rides during these treatments, though he needed to keep his skin covered to reduce his sun exposure. He also started wearing a bandana. Unfortunately, the news quickly went from bad to worse as his doctors also discovered that he had a brain tumor. He needed a custom medical helmet fitted so doctors could deliver focused radiation directly to his head.

On June 10, I received the worst phone call of my life. Jimmy had died. I was in shock. I had just seen him a few days before, and he seemed fine. I was afraid of what my life would become without Jimmy. He had always believed in me and had always been there for me, from the time I was in Little League through several breakups and even while dealing with my mental illness.

Now he was gone. I ran outside to the side porch at my parents' house, crying uncontrollably. My parents came out to see what was wrong, and I had to force the words out so they could understand. They were upset and tried to hug and comfort me, but I just felt like I needed to be left alone. After about twenty minutes, it dawned on me that this was the first time in over a year that I'd been able to cry. I made a vow to Jimmy that I would stop taking my medications cold turkey.

In my mind, there were only two possible outcomes, and I accepted them both: 1) I would die, as the doctors had warned was a possibility, and be reunited with Jimmy, or 2) I would be able to return to work and resume living a normal life. In the meantime, I offered up a prayer to God. "If you want to take me, I'm yours," I said. "I don't want to suffer like this, and if I'm to stay, I won't take or need those medications anymore."

I couldn't tell my parents about this decision because of what my dad had said about the consequences. I couldn't even tell my counselor, Mr. Connor. At that point, I was still on 800 milligrams of Thorazine a day, and I knew it would take about two or three weeks for this to get out of my system. I made sure to throw away my daily dose each day so there would be no evidence that I hadn't taken them.

Summer 1986

Three weeks after Jimmy's death and my decision to eliminate my medication, I received another phone call, this time from my friend Todd Nelson, whom we called Woody. A buddy from high school, Woody and I used to ride our motorcycles to and from school and went to a lot of keg parties together. He told me the company he worked for needed help demolishing a house damaged by fire in the city. The contractor who was going to rebuild the site needed the original structure removed before they could begin work. I decided to give it a try and see if I could function at a job now that I was off my meds.

When I arrived on site, Woody handed me a pry bar and a hammer, and thus began another big life journey with an even bigger destination. We tore down the old, burned-out house, leaving only the first-floor deck, which was still in good shape and sitting on a solid foundation. From here, I got a second chance in life and a new career. I worked hard for my friend Woody, and as I helped demo that house, I began to rebuild my life.

About a week later, Woody told me I was doing good work and just might be able to get a job as a carpenter with the contractors who were going to rebuild the house — Dave and Bud LaMantia of Homescapes. It felt like a dream come true. It was as if I were waking up from the darkest, longest nightmare I'd ever experienced. I had lost a year of my life to the mental health care system, and now I was handed this wonderful opportunity.

Even though I knew very little about carpentry up until that point, I put forth my best effort and found that I could develop a great passion for the daily tasks set before me. They gave me a massive boost of energy and, even though I was getting paid, my main reward was learning a trade I could carry with me for the rest of my life.

I had found a new passion. Over time, I taught myself to read again by poring over the construction blueprints for the new house. I learned to read mechanical instructions for different hardware — locks, doors, and so on. I was like a sponge, eager to absorb as much new information as I possibly could. Within a year and a half, Dave LaMantia had given me a beautiful four-foot wooden level to symbolize my rite of passage as a carpenter, and he made me foreman of my own crew. I hired my best friends, and together we worked and played hard.

We built two 3,000-square-foot houses at the end of a cul-de-sac near the neighborhood where I grew up. In the back of my Chilton auto repair manual, I found an ad for a book on house construction. I ordered it and used it as a guide during these construction projects, sometimes reading up on procedures the night before we did them. I read very slowly because reading was an emotionally trying process for me; my passion for building gave me the courage to continue. I don't think my coworkers were aware of my reading difficulty because I hid it so well.

I also ran a $1.5 million job to construct SKF-MRC's global sales offices. This project was the feather in my cap during my three years working with Homescapes. It was also the project that got me offered a job as a journeyman carpenter with Scalise Construction in Local Union 66 without having to serve an apprenticeship.

Thanks to landing that job with Dave and Bud, I had many great learning experiences, and they allowed me to get into the Carpenters Union as a journeyman at such a young age.

It was almost surreal. I had come through the depths of despair and reclaimed my life.

Afterword

"Love — it is God: the unity within oneness, with no separation, no judgment, no conditions."

- Kurt B. Johnson

Rising With the Lone Star: Charged by Choice

Forty years ago, on that starry summer night beside the swimming pool in Dallas, everything changed. I slipped into a deep hypnotic meditation as I focused on that single star in the night sky. I began contemplating a simple question that had haunted me since childhood: "Do I go to church out of love — or do I go to church out of fear?"

I sat in silence, reflecting on how fear and love have shaped my life — from choosing to go to church or stay away, to my passion for diving tempered by the fear of those difficult dives, and to that motorcycle accident: crashing at more than 100 miles an hour alongside a barbed wire fence that could have sliced me in half. Yet just days later, I got back on the bike and took the same corner.

Suddenly, there at the pool, I slipped into a state free of fear. I experienced an authentic love — an absence of fear, a state of being outside of emotion. It was oneness beyond words, a pure presence. In that moment, I moved past mere experience into the home of all-knowing — needing nothing, not even a thought, feeling, or emotion. I lacked for nothing. Since then, I've been able to return to this state at times, flowing in and out like an ocean tide or an electrical current — the outgoing and the return. I occasionally experience three-night stretches without sleep, each bringing grand insights. The aftershocks of these sleepless nights disrupt my life for weeks, if not months. These experiences became the foundation of my Experiential Philosophy — *The Energy Within ME* — and the core topics of *Mindful Mondays,* videos available on my social media outlets.

Within this state of love — not an emotion, but a pure state of being — I touched my true essence. It was an authentic love, far above ordinary emotional love: without judgment or conditions. As I held my focus on that pinpoint of light from the star, in the deep silence, an image emerged: a battery.

One pole glowed with golden warmth: Love (+)

The other dull silver and cold: Fear (–)

In that instant, I understood:

Life's Electric, Stupid!

Please don't be triggered by the word *stupid.* It's part of the hard-earned wisdom from the School of Hard Knocks, where you've got to be tough if you're going to be stupid—or else learn to make smarter choices.

Life's electric, stupid! Two invisible currents power everything we feel, think, and do.

From that night forward, I have been trying, often clumsily, to speak a language the world may not have heard yet. This book is the result of four decades of living and nearly fifteen years of concentrated writing. What began as an infallible glimpse has become Experiential Philosophy: a practical, lived path that treats every moment of life as the only classroom you'll ever need.

The curriculum is relentless but straightforward: Notice which pole you're plugged into right now, Love (+) or Fear (–), and choose again.

This choice is about using your emotional intelligence to align with a higher, authentic intelligence — not the artificial kind. The original intelligence running in your body and soul since the day you were born. It speaks to us with a binary language of pluses and minuses, stored in your physiology through the mind-body connection.

When you learn to read that language, fear stops being your enemy and becomes data — raw, honest data saying *This is not what I want.* The discomfort becomes the returning current, guiding you back into love.

Experiential Philosophy aligns with the teachings of the Hermetica, a collection of ancient philosophical and mystical texts attributed to Hermes Trismegistus. In their book, *The Lost Wisdom of the Pharaohs,* Timothy Freke and Peter Gandy highlight a key idea from the Hermetica: "Man is a marvel." This concept reflects the belief that human beings possess a unique potential to transcend their ordinary nature and awaken their divine essence. According to Hermes, the purpose of human life is to realize this divine potential and achieve a deeper connection with the divine, fulfilling God's greatest desire for humanity.

I use the term *Binary Harmetics* to describe this binary operating system of Love (+) and Fear (-). It doesn't ask you to deny fear or rise above it. It asks only this: feel the fear fully, recognize it for what it is — "I do not want this" — and pivot your mindset toward the natural opposite, the love you truly want.

That pivot is courage.

That pivot is freedom.

That pivot is the entire spiritual path.

Love, in its ultimate sense, has no opposites. It is not an emotion that comes and goes — it is the unchanging ground of being, the ocean beneath all the waves. Human love is the wave: beautiful, conditional, and sometimes stormy. Divine love, or what I've learned to call *the ocean,* is eternal, impersonal, and already present.

The game of our lifetime is to let the wave of personal love arise inside the ocean that is never threatened by what is happening on the surface. That underlying ocean is your true self — authentic love, not the fleeting emotion.

We are waves rising from that ocean, yet fear often tricks us into believing we are separate. The wave takes control, becoming the master of the soul, while the soul forgets its power and becomes a slave to the form.

But the truth is the reverse: the soul is the master of the wave, for it is the ocean experiencing itself in wave form. You are both the ocean and the wave.

The essence of the ocean is love. You are a wave in a sea of love. Fear creates the illusion of separation — letting us feel cut off, lost in the crash and foam, forgetting our authentic essence is love. Too often, we accept this illusion, too lazy — or too afraid — to look deeper and remember: we never left the ocean at all.

Consider the story of Jesus and his disciples crossing the Sea of Galilee. A violent storm suddenly arose, waves crashing over the boat, and the disciples — seasoned fishermen — panicked, convinced they were about to drown. Meanwhile, Jesus slept peacefully in the stern. In desperation, they woke him, crying, "Teacher, don't you care if we drown?" He rose, rebuked the wind, and said to the waves, "Quiet! Be still!" Instantly, the storm ceased, and the sea grew completely calm.

The disciples were left in awe, asking, "Who is this? Even the wind and the waves obey him!" In that moment, Jesus embodied the undisturbed ocean of love beneath the chaos — showing that the true master does not fight the wave but commands it from the stillness within.

Just as Jesus calmed the storm from inner stillness, we calm our waves by choosing the ocean beneath. Fear is the only thing that appears to separate us from that ocean — yet the discomfort caused by that fear is the only thing capable of returning us to it.

Just like a battery: the outgoing charge and the return charge are the same current. Separation and return. Sin (missing the mark) and redemption. Death and resurrection. It's all electricity doing what electricity does.

And just as the ocean is a vast body of water, so are we. Our bodies are roughly 70% water, vessels where physical matter intersects with the spirit realm. Our emotions ripple through that inner sea, creating invisible waves we feel in every cell.

What You Think About, You Bring About.

First comes the breath — being charged positively or negatively, then the word. The word becomes a thought, and contemplating that thought becomes a feeling. Holding onto that feeling becomes an emotion.

Negative words that lead to negative thinking lead to negative experiences. Your negative thinking leads to doubting anything positive. It becomes an addiction. It becomes a fear-based prison.

Alan Watts, a popular philosopher in the 1960s counterculture movement, said, "Addictions are a result of a spiritual crisis."

These spiritual crises stem from choosing fear over love. These negative thought addictions sometimes express themselves in your body as disease. Alcoholism is a spiritual crisis in physical form — an immaterial crisis expressing itself in the material world, seeking yourself outside of yourself.

Victimhood is another example of a spiritual crisis. Living in a state of perpetual victimhood separates us from our true, authentic, intelligent selves. Victimhood is a fear-based falsehood used to entrap us. Our leaders use victimhood to enslave us. They use the fear of victimization to control us by enticing us to seek protection outside of ourselves from an institution such as the government.

Fear-based control — like making everyone feel like a victim in our society — twists the advertising principles Wed Howard taught me into something darker.

People want to feel safe.

People want to look and feel good.

People want to feel protected.

Eleanor Roosevelt said, “Nobody can make you feel inferior without your consent.” If the government, religion, or a person is attempting to protect you and win your vote through censorship or the restriction of freedom of speech, remember, no words can make you feel anything without your consent.

The antidote for a spiritual crisis is simply choosing love over fear.

Energy in Motion

Emotions shape the state of our body of water — calm or stormy. Your spirit is the actual pilot of this vessel. When you let spirit lead, the all-knowing mind becomes the autopilot — guiding you effortlessly through the waves, back to unity and love. The body becomes the co-pilot of your spirit, using emotional intelligence to navigate.

When you choose to allow fear to slip away, as if you are Teflon, instead of choosing to let it stick to you like Velcro — when you greet every constriction from separation with curiosity, welcoming it instead of judging it — you discover something astonishing: you do not have to wait for heaven.

We’ve had it backwards for thousands of years: mind, body, spirit. It’s time we move spirit to the front of the bus, the driver’s seat, allowing spirit to be the captain of the ship! Spirit, mind, body. We experience spirit through thoughts and feelings based on the words we choose to contemplate.

Allow your spirit to be the pilot of the vessel. Connect your mind with your body through your thoughts and feelings by choosing love over fear. Your body autocorrects in this state of love, without fear. Heal the spiritual crisis with your thoughts and feelings, and your physical health autocorrects.

You become the temple of *I AM Love.*

Your body is the temple of choice (love) or the temple of chance (fear).

Most people shut down before they even contemplate — convinced they already know the answer, too lazy to look deeper. But contemplation is the key to our survival.

It's not easy. That's why so few do it.

As Carl Jung said, "Thinking is difficult, that's why most people judge."

Critical thinking ends with judgment.

Contemplation is thinking on steroids — it creates our *U-iverse.* Robert Edward Grant coined the term *U-iverse* to describe how the universe is a perfect reflection of our inner selves. Our internal emotional and mental states don't just shape our experience — they mirror the external world.

When we contemplate deeply, we see the connection.

We stop judging.

We start choosing.

Life Is Choice, Because It's Always Changing

Life never stands still. Every moment brings new circumstances, emotions, challenges, and opportunities — an endless flow of change. In that constant flux, we are never passive victims. We always have the freedom and the responsibility to choose how we respond. Because it's always changing, no situation is permanent. Pain passes. Joy shifts. Relationships evolve. Opportunities arise and fade. These situations are not permanent.

Life is choice because in every shifting moment, we decide which current to follow: Love (+) or Fear (–). We can react with contraction (fear, avoidance, judgment) or expansion (love, courage, curiosity).

Change creates the space for choice. Without change, we become stuck in a static loop. But because life moves relentlessly and unpredictably, each new wave gives us another chance to pivot toward love.

The outgoing current (separation, fear) and the return current (realignment, love) are the same energy. Change is the movement. Choice is how we direct it.

In practice, it looks like this:

A setback hits (change). You feel fear rise. Instead of resisting or collapsing, you pause, notice the charge, and choose compassion over criticism, action over avoidance, connection over isolation.

Your choices charge you — positively or negatively.

Not choosing is still a choice — like playing Russian roulette.

Choosing mindfulness is a skill, while choosing nothing is a game of chance.

I am choosing free will!

Once you've tasted that state of authentic love, returning becomes easier. Whether you read the words of Jesus, Buddha, Muhammad, Hermes, or any mystic or enlightened teacher, try this simple shift: replace the word GOD with LOVE.

For millennia, religious leaders and institutions have weaponized the name of God to control people through fear — dividing them with threats of wrath, exclusion, or eternal punishment, all in the name of a deity defined by judgment rather than compassion. Yet God's true nature, as revealed across traditions, is Love itself.

Suppose we all made that replacement — seeing Love where "God" once stood. The fear-based control that has gripped humanity for millennia would crumble overnight. Wars over doctrine, guilt over sin, and divisions over whose God is right — all would lose their power.

For two thousand years, many Christian churches have crucified the very law of love that Jesus taught — his own words of compassion, forgiveness, and unity twisted into tools of judgment and exclusion. Jesus himself railed against the religious authorities of his time, calling out how they bastardized the word of God with rigid rules and hypocrisy. For that, they crucified him. And yet, today, many churches do the same to his teachings: turning messages of radical love into fear-mongering dogma that separates rather than unites.

Know that God is Love, and you will return to that authentic intelligent love faster, without the fear-based separation of wondering whose God is right or wrong.

I will choose LOVE!

In this physical form — right here, right now, in this breathing, imperfect, glorious body — you are already home, and you have an early warning system to let you know when you are out of alignment with your authentic, intelligent self. Use this data from the discomfort from fear to help you reconnect to love. It's an information system, a language.

The forgiveness of fear is simply a return to love. Whether you created the separation from love or someone else did, the forgiveness of fear allows the negative current of judgment to flow through you like Teflon and not stick to you like Velcro. Forgiving the action of fear is simply a return to love.

Forgive me of my fears, as I forgive those who have feared against me. Lead me not into the temptation of fear, but also deliver me from the evils of fear.

Love is oneness with God!

Feel everything — but do not believe any story that says you are small. Love fiercely — but need nothing back. When fear shows up (and it will), smile like you're greeting an old friend who forgot the way home.

Place your hands together — in a sacred sigil formed by two hands in a gesture of love and unity — fingers gracefully extended and interlocked (as shown on the cover of this book). A heart shape emerges between the palms, the center of emotional truth. A pyramid rises from the wrists, symbolizing grounded spiritual ascent. A temple silhouette crowns the hands, representing the inner sanctuary of wisdom. On the cover — a lone star shines through the apex — symbolizing divine destiny, the guiding light of purpose. Meditate with this sigil to align your intentions with love and higher purpose.

This book is not a destination; it's a poolside invitation to choose love over fear in every moment. Contemplating every choice without judgment and allowing fear to align you with Love.

LOVE is the energy within ME!

With Love and Light,
Kurt B. Johnson

Living by Choice

Driven by hands-on experience, Kurt B. Johnson learns by doing. He's worked as a carpenter, started businesses, and owns a restaurant and club. His Experiential Philosophy introduces *Binary Harmetics*, a new way of thinking that views emotions as data and information — pathways to harmony or signals of disorder. His first book, *Lone Star Rising*, tells of his motorcycle ride to Texas at 18 — a story of family, legacy, and building things that last.

At 19, Kurt opened his first business: Advanced Auto Tint in Dallas, Texas, with the slogan "You've Got It Made in the Shade." His mentor, Wed Howard — former announcer of *The Ed Sullivan Show* — taught him advertising basics and supplied the memorable tagline.

This photo was taken in the summer of 1994, just months before Kurt signed the lease to build Shawbucks. In 1995, at age 29, he opened the restaurant and music venue in Jamestown, New York — constructing it from the ground up after a fire had destroyed the previous building on the site. The name honors his great-uncle Clarence "Shawbuck" Olsen, a World War II medic who rode trains across the country. Clarence's resilience lives on in Shawbucks.

Two weeks after signing the lease for Shawbucks, he was diagnosed with testicular cancer. He underwent treatment while building the restaurant, holding on to this belief: "The only bad experience in life is the one you didn't learn from." That mindset helped him heal and keep going.

Kurt met his wife Tammy in 1997. Married in 2001, they have two sons: Colin, now running Shawbucks, and Kaden, a nursing student and hockey player. Shawbucks remains central to their family legacy.

Today, Kurt and his family run Shawbucks and live in Jamestown. He is working on his second book, *Unstoppable AI: Charting the Path Between Artificial and Authentic Intelligence.*

www.ingramcontent.com/pod-product-compliance
Lightning Source LLC
LaVergne TN
LVHW090527110826
845146LV00003B/1004

* 9 7 9 8 9 9 5 1 2 1 7 0 1 *